GEORGE MORE

A
WAY
TO
GOD

ENABLING AND SHARING IN INDIA

By
Mary More

Edited by
Ron Ferguson

1

First   Published   1991

The Wild Goose is a Celtic symbol of the Holy Spirit
It is the Trademark   of Wild Goose Publications

WILD GOOSE PUBLICATIONS
The Publishing   Division   of The Iona Community
Pearce Institute,   840 Govan Road, Glasgow G51 3UU
Tel. (041) 445 4561   Fax. (041) 445 4295

Printed in Great Britain by
Billing & Sons Ltd, Worcester

Contents

We gratefully acknowledge the contribution of the Drummond Trust, 3 Pitt Terrace, Stirling towards the publication costs of this book.

Dedicated

with love and gratitude

to

Janet and Alex

who took it all in their stride

and to

Rev. Wm. Stewart, B.D., D.D.,

George's early colleague who read

the manuscript a few days before he died.

Editor's Introduction

George More was one of the wisest — and holiest — men I have ever met.

To say someone is 'holy' can be to mark him or her down as a pain in the neck. The picture conjured up is often that of a person overconcerned with religious observance, and before whom one has to hold one's breath and whisper. Not so with George. He was the perfect model of what Dietrich Bonhoeffer called 'holy worldliness' — that characteristic which enjoys the world to the full while, at the same time, entering into its pain, sustained all the time by an arcane and utterly unobtrusive discipline.

George More was a saint who didn't have much time for religion and all its works. He could not be bothered with ecclesiastical paraphernalia. His devotion was to Jesus Christ who, George was convinced, did not intend to found yet another religion, but rather to provide a Way to God and to true humanity. This Way could be used by people of differing religious outlooks, while still retaining their own distinctive observances.

George was deadly serious about ultimate things, but very laid back and humorous about what he considered to be less than ultimate matters. He delivered radical, and sometimes outrageous, ideas in such amusing, unpretentious and benign ways that one had to pinch oneself and ask whether one had heard him aright. As a counsellor and pastor he was immensely wise, caring and skilful, and people in need homed in on him, knowing that they would receive unconditional yet unsentimental and rigorous love. Indian terms are very appropriate for George. He was a guru, albeit a quiet, Presbyterian one; and, as Walter Fyfe observes, he could well be described as a Mahatma, great soul. A great 'Indian' soul with a Scottish chortle.

Mary More began the task of writing this memoir as a kind of therapy — but the therapy only worked because the task was crying out to be done. Her manuscript, which was originally much longer and more detailed, provides a remarkable portrait of an exceptional man at work. It is also a story of a rich Scottish Presbyterian tradition which has all but died — the making of a missionary to India by way of local kirk, University, Student Christian Movement, theological college and the mission field itself.

Mary's book understandably plays down her own role. Yet the reader should know that Mary was an equal partner; indeed, the syllables 'GeorgeandMary' tended to be operated as one word, so inseparable were they. Mary's affectionate memoir of her 'other half' (rather than her 'better half') is both a touching and perceptive tribute to George, and a worthy addition to the literature about missionary work in India.

Ron Ferguson.
Iona, November 1990

Introduction

For many years George had been under pressure to write about his work in India. Pressure came early from the Christian Institute for the Study of Religion and Society, Bangalore and this continued into his retiral years. He continually postponed making a definite commitment to undertake this, though friends kept hoping that he would eventually do it. The desire to see this account of his work seemed sincere and reasonable, and I had been very convinced that he should do it and encouraged him all I could. So when George died I wondered if I should attempt it.

I was greatly encouraged, and later confirmed in my decision, by finding amongst George's papers evidence that he had certainly given the matter consideration. He left some very helpful material, much of which appears here as it stands. Some of it has afforded me help and guidance in areas in which I lacked competence.

George's main life work developed in the Indian village of Allipur in Maharashtra, some twenty miles from Wardha and from Sevagram, where Mahatma Gandhi had set up his Ashram. However, it seemed to me that any account of these 30 years would be incomplete unless accompanied by some history of his early life and preparation, and also of the variety of service he contributed in these ten years of "retirement".

In thinking over the form this might take, I remembered

9

how frequently George described the idea of the four asramas in Hindu philosophy — the Four Stages of Life.

First	**Bramacarya**	the period of discipline, training and education.
Second	**Garhasthya**	the period of the householder, the active worker.
Third	**Vanaprasthya**	a period of detachment from the responsibilities of the second stage and the opportunity to share (and in George's case, to develop) accumulated interests and wisdom of the years.
Fourth	**Sannyasa**	at the hermit life period the analogy falls down! — George would have continued to enjoy the Third stage as he was living it.

Without making too great point of it, George's life does fall naturally into these three stages.

Mary More.

Stage 1 – Bramacarya

The Child Is Father Of The Man

– Wordsworth

It is a kind of humorous, humble, self-effacing secrecy of devotion and hope which finds no counterpart in the visible world, nothing in symbol or gesture by which it may be fully reflected or expressed. Nevertheless, it is there and the simplicities of the Gospel, the call to be humble and unostentatious in prayer, never using naked power but always service and sacrifice, are both its sustenance and its preservative.

R. Gregor Smith – expounding Bonhoeffer's meaning of a distinctively Christian style of life.

It is a mark of great wisdom not to be moved by every kind of words; for thus we shall go on securely in the course we have begun.

Thomas a Kempis.

Beware of making a fetish of consistency to your convictions instead of being devoted to God.

Oswald Chambers.

The poets were able to tell us long before the enlightenment of the science of Psychology – but Psychology is God's gift, and it is good to have the confirmation. One of the greatest influences for good in this childhood fathering of the man is to be part of a large family. In this George More was greatly blessed in having three brothers and, when he was 13, a sister. To have firstly an experience of community and secondly, such close early association with babyhood, probably influenced George in his quick response to the concept of community in many different forms, and his remarkable rapport with infants and young children. His concern for the sick, and his interest in medicine, may have stemmed from the fact that his father was crippled by a stroke when George, the oldest of the family, was only about

12 years old. His father died when George was about 16 years old. In the intervening years, he saw his mother's acceptance, care and nursing of his father.

The most powerful influence in his early life was his mother, whose courage and steadiness of purpose were matched only by her faith as she faced the years of nursing in addition to bringing up five children — and, after her husband's death, the managing of the family finances.

The influence of his father was more mixed. He was of the stern stuff often associated with Scottish parents — sparing of encouragement and approval and producing in George, as in so many offspring of similar parents, an unwarranted sense of inadequacy, vulnerability and lack of self-confidence. Those who knew him knew that George overcame these handicaps sufficiently to make a strong, positive contribution in life, but he never attained to the sense of satisfaction in what he accomplished that one would have liked him to have.

Further childhood influence "fathering" George towards the man he became were the Church and the manifold activities of a very alive and active congregation, good ministry, choir and Sunday School — where he was assistant leader of the Primary department.

In the large and famous Boys' Brigade Company (69th Glasgow), there was training in camping and climbing, map reading and swimming, outdoors and inside gymnastics, music, production of Gilbert and Sullivan operas, playing in the orchestra and latterly conducting — all in addition to the basic Bible and character training.

In home, in school and in the Boys' Brigade there was encouragement for George to develop the musical gift he possessed, and at Glasgow University he greatly enjoyed singing in the student choir. He played the violin and the cello and even had a "go" at the double bass! But there was above all the steady thread of his singing voice, a source of real pleasure to his associates throughout his whole life.

When it came time for George to come towards a decision about his choice of a life's work, he was uncertain. Pressed by both his mother and the B. B. Captain to consider the ministry of the Church, he resisted, because he did not like the general image of the job; and, from lack of any obvious alternative, he decided to take up an apprenticeship in accountancy in the family business of Norman D. Sloan in Glasgow.

Professor Forrester of St. Mary's College, St. Andrews, was wont to question new students about the place of illness, if any, in their lives and especially whether such an illness had influenced their choice of a career. Professor Forrester was himself of the opinion that, in many cases, students had been influenced in decisions during a longish illness.

In fact, about this time, in his middle teens, George had a series of serious illnesses, necessitating his absence from school for nearly a year. He used the given time to read a great deal, but mostly he listened to music on the radio and began a serious study of the theory of music. Dr. Forrester would not have found any immediate change of direction, and certainly no move towards the ministry during this spell of illness.

However, it is likely that much that was deeply influential in his life's work was seeded in that time. During this accountancy period George continued his very full church programme. About the end of his third year in this course, he had a further spell confined to bed as the result of a leg injury in a minor climbing accident.

It was in these weeks that George began to face the fact that he had become increasingly unhappy about the prospect of life as an accountant, and to doubt his ability and calling for this work. Gradually he found himself looking again at the ministry as a possible avenue for the kind of service and work to which he felt himself called.

The way to such a change was by no means clear for him. Mainly there was the matter of prolonging the cost of education for himself while there were four other members of the family to follow. After much thought, he approached his mother. Her answer was that he must change to the long course for the ministry and she would manage.

After discussion with the minister of Ruchill Church and with Rev. George Docherty, another Ruchill man, George became a full time student in the Arts faculty at Glasgow University in 1935 and a candidate for the ministry.

George spent much of his free time in the Students Union, the International Club, and the Student Christian Movement. He was also involved in political discussions, playing his violin, singing, resuscitating the Sino-Scottish

Society, making friends, and thinking through ideas in politics, society and religion. He **did** have to read and write essays in his chosen subjects — philosophy, political economy, education and Russian — but a lot of his education came from discussion with fellow students. He was introduced very forcefully to the Indian Independence Movement, sometimes in the very practical way of taking part in "round table" discussions, where the Indian students played the part of members of the British Government and officials, and the Scottish students the Indian leaders. At one time George played M. K. Gandhi! These occasions were much enjoyed but were, in addition, learning experiences which enabled him, some ten years later, to begin his life and work in India with a head start in understanding Indian politics.

George's intimate association with the Student Christian Movement all through his University years played a vital part in the development of his faith and in the shaping of his life. The S. C. M. condition of membership was — "A desire to understand the Christian faith and to live the Christian life". No doubts or questions prevented a student from joining the movement, but in the leadership and in committee members, a core of sound faith was necessary.

Missionary speakers at S. C. M. meetings and study groups had their own special message and challenge, but in the end it was a very personal challenge that brought George to see that he should take part in the overseas mission of the Church. An African student pointed out to George that here in the West there were one or more churches at every street corner, while in his country, churches and ministers were few and far between — so why hang around here? George, getting the point, became a student volunteer missionary.

(It seems that as a young child I had announced I was going to be a missionary. A cousin told me she had been sent to bring me home from Sunday School and I had told her this. What **could** I have had in mind? Anyway I had maintained this conviction and was already in the Student Volunteer Missionary Union when George joined it. I joined it to see if I could find out what I meant!)

George had a brief spell of holiday on Iona at the end of August 1939 — having graduated M. A. — where he took a long look at the likely changes ahead, returning several days before war was declared on September 3rd, 1939. He had accepted the offer of a job as S. C. M. Travelling Secretary for the coming academic year before beginning his theological course. The expected reduction in student numbers necessitated a curtailment in S. C. M. staff and it was suggested to George that he night begin his theological studies in St. Mary's College, St. Andrews while undertaking a part-time S. C. M. Secretaryship, travelling between St. Andrews, Dundee and Aberdeen. In the gloom and uncertainty prevailing then, this was a welcome arrangement, allowing him part-time work and the privilege he greatly appreciated of studying under Donald Baillie at St. Mary's.

On a more personal note, George and I became engaged to be married on September 3rd, 1939, before going to church and hearing war declared! Many will realise that this engagement was in the proper S. C. M. tradition of Students Carefully Matched — or — the Society for Courtship and Marriage!

It became clear after several months of what was known as the "phoney war", that there was to be little movement in the junior medical job circle and the Church of Scotland Foreign Mission Committee invited me to fill a missionary vacancy in the Mure Memorial Hospital in Nagpur in Central India for three years. The two most concerned in this decision were eased towards it by remembering that one doesn't put one's hand to the plough and look back — so we travelled together to Liverpool to embark me on the Anchor Line *Britannia*.

In the event, the time in St. Andrews for George was to prove to be one year only, but it was a very full, hard-working and interesting year. In this time of "phoney war" George found his life very full and exciting. He laid the foundation of his theological studies and began to learn the S. C. M. job. The basic work went on — meeting students, arranging study groups, retreats and hikes, as he travelled between St. Andrews, Dundee and Aberdeen, encouraging, advising, setting up committees, and looking out for leadership.

George's closest friends at this time were Bob Craig and James Devine. Together they struggled with the war problem. Pacifism began to take on a different aspect. As Divinity students thay had optional military reservation — no courts, no appeals, no hassle, no agonising cost, just reservation "on a plate". Why should it be so easy for them? Where were their own generation? Where was the mission field now? One day George went into a cinema to try to come to a decision.

The lights went up and there was James Devine sitting beside him, on the same quest. They went out and talked it to a conclusion. Their place was to be with the men of their own generation: the place to be a missionary was in the forces. They volunteered for the Gordon Highlanders.

Eventually George took the advice of his officers and applied for a commission, in the Artillery. He did his officer's training in Wales and, finding the need at that time in the Coastal Command, was posted to Orkney.

I came home at the end of my three years in India and we were married at my home church in Prestwick. Bob Craig was best man. I don't remember the details very much, but I heard the minister praying a blessing on our "baskets and our cupboards". How did he know I was very proud of my baskets?!

George being an officer, we were entitled to first class railway tickets — to Troon! They cost 5 pence (old pennies) each and were in George's uniform pocket at the end of the war!

* * * * * * *

Now we were into the long haul of the last two years of the war. We entered this almost ashamed of our joy — of the safety of our family, for George's three brothers were alive in the services.

The brief leaves shine out like stars in these two years. When we were both free we went to our family homes in Glasgow and Prestwick — once we danced through both the afternoon and evening sessions of the Glasgow Plaza!

Then on to Hiroshima. We were stunned with the horror of it — little knowing then the nuclear arms build-up that was ahead of us — stunned and horror-stricken, and yet it was the end of the war.

George was demobbed promptly, privileged as a student. An effort was being made to get students back to their classes for the beginning of the session in 1945. We had a home to go to in Bell Street in St. Andrews, in which to live what was probably the most peaceful two years of our life — in which Janet was born, and George completed his B. D. course.

I best remember the S. C. M. Study Groups held in our sitting room at 5 Bell Street — though my memories lack detail of the discussion, one eye being on the play pen and half of my mind wondering if there would be enough pancakes for the coffee after! However I know we were putting down the thought-roots of missionary theology and policy and cementing still more S. C. M. friendships to last us our life time.

George was greatly influenced by the Dutch missionary and theologian Henrik Kraemer and he twice underlined the following quotation from Kraemer's book *The Christian Message in a Non-Christian World* —

"The remarkable paradox in the life of every religious worker who is called to recommend the Gospel to the consciences of men is that it is his plain obligation and privilege to exert himself to the utmost and to utilise every means that experience and knowledge and talent put at his disposal, seemingly working as if all depended on his sincere devotion to the task; and yet that he has to be deeply and reverently aware that it is 'God who makes the seed grow', and that only 'The Day will show what the nature of his work is'. This paradox produces a deep tranquillity and at the same time opens the way for a humorous modesty in regards to one's work."

Yet George did not go all the way with Kraemer's Barthian position (Kraemer himself was later to change, much to George's joy). George did not like Christian exclusivism, which he saw as opposed to the essential spirit of Jesus. I want to record as correctly as I can remember it a saying of George's that I have heard him propound on several occasions:-

"In the cesspool of Europe, enclosed by seas and unknown lands of barbarian hordes and others of Muslim Moors, the Christian Church sat in councils and composed the Christian doctrine; in complete ignorance of all that the rest of the world might contain of God's actions amongst his children in India and China and the peoples of all the islands of the seas, and this restricted message — this new exclusive religion — was eventually preached throughout the world as the definitive Christian Gospel".

* * * * * * *

For George the period of Bramacarya, the active period of education, discipline and hard work, finally ended in the summer of 1947 when he graduated B. D. from St. Andrews University with medals in Divinity and Ecclesiastical history. He was appointed by the Foreign Mission to be a District

Missionary in the Nagpur (India) area. In Martyr's Church, St. Andrews, on June 30th, 1947, he received his ordination to this missionary ministry.

In a sense, running parallel with these three clinching events, another memorable and far-reaching decision was made. George liked to tell the story of the definitive culmination of this process. His connection with the Iona Community had begun almost with the beginning of the Community itself. He had spent periods on the island from the two weeks immediately before the onset of the war, right through his first St. Andrews year, the long army years and again during the two final study years at St. Mary's. Some time during this last period, as George recounted, he was accompanying George MacLeod to a meeting with St. Mary's men. George MacLeod asked George why, despite his constant relationship with the Community, he had never applied for membership. Of course the answer was quite simple; as soon as the B. D. course was finished, the More family would sail for India, so there was no time for George to carry out the necessary two year programme for full membership of the Community. At this point, my George was wont to say, "We walked from the end of Howard Place along Market Street to this stone, and George MacLeod stopped and pronounced: 'Columba's was an overseas missionary movement, and the Iona Community will also be so. You, George, will be our first overseas missionary member. It will be sufficient if you spend the summer on the island'." . . . . and so it was.

Discipline, education and hard work are somewhat unexciting, dry words to describe and contain all that George put into these full years, but on thinking on the meaning and content of these words, they do seem able to include and comprehend that mini-lifetime called Bramacarya.

Stage Two — Garhasthya

I feel the winds of God today
Today my sail I lift,
Though heavy oft with drenching spray
And torn with many a rift;
If hope but light the water's crest
And Christ my bark will use,
I'll seek the seas at his behest
And brave another cruise.

The Christian is not a religious person, but simply a human being, as Jesus was a human being . . . profoundly this-worldly, characterised by discipline and the constant knowledge of death and resurrection.

Dietrich Bonhoeffer.

Q. What did that really mean, being present in the world?

A. It meant you had to go and live as a priest, someone who had been trained in religion, among the people, and especially among the working class people. You did not have to talk about God and the Church but just be there, among people, in the hope that they would become aware of something — a deeper mystery — because of your Christian praxis, your way of life. The strategy of being present in the world has to awaken in others the religious questions, and to do that by your way of life.

Edward Schillebeeckx.

I have all my missionary life been very conscious and appreciative of the undoubted privilege, comfort and general graciousness of the voyages to and from India (and I am sad for all the young travellers of these days who by and large must travel by air and will never know this great privilege).

Although it was 1947, our voyage was still organised under wartime conditions. The ship was a captured German vessel re-named *Empire Trooper*. George shared a cabin with five men and I was one iron companion-way further into the bowels of the ship, with toddler Janet (one and a half years), and Alex already making his presence felt, I never knew whether I was seasick or morning-sick, or a combination of both.

Each morning we went on deck and George fastened Janet into her reins and proceeded to walk the deck for most of the day, on the end of the baby reins. I sought somewhere to sit and steady my internal confusion. However, there were no chairs on deck and one sat precariously on wooden chests and took what reassurance one could from the knowledge of the life jackets contained therein!

The voyage took four weeks instead of the customary two weeks or so because we were, mainly in the Red Sea, taken off course to call in at various ports to set down and pick up military personnel.

But we arrived at Bombay, and it was Dewali! — the Festival of Lights (and great noise). We had begun our missionary life, we were together in India. In our Glasgow student days we had both become student volunteer missionaries but that was a very full twelve years behind us; and so it really was a profound experience to find "We had made it". What we would make **of** it, we had no way of knowing. Our immediate problems were the practical ones associated with luggage and offices and train reservations. These were all greatly alleviated by the caring missionary community in Bombay in those days, so that with their help we eventually set off on the fifteen hour journey to Nagpur.

We lived in Nagpur for two years while George studied the Marathi language. During my first years I had studied Hindi and passed the first missionary exam; but, as a wife, Marathi study was not available to me! The end result was that George spoke Marathi as someone speaking Inverness English, while my 'picked up' Marathi was rather like broad Glasgow English — but it sufficed!

While George's main work was language study — and the practice of it so important — it was not easy in a city community of educated Christians all anxious to practise their English! George attended Presbytery meetings and Standing Committee (Session) meetings. Bill Stewart, his senior colleague, and he discussed at length the division of their work and how it should develop.

Leslie Newbiggin had said around this time that, where

20

the situation was appropriate, a missionary might offer to stand for a call to an Indian congregation, and this attracted George very much. In the event the church in the town of Wardha, some fifty miles south of Nagpur, fell vacant, and it was suggested to them that they might consider calling George. They seemed happy — perhaps a little surprised — with the idea and did indeed call him in true Presbyterian style. He was inducted to the charge in November 1949.

Shortly before this, George had passed his second language examination, but even the second exam pass does not make a Marathi linguist of the student. It showed considerable courage for George to undertake his first parish experience in a foreign language, dealing with all the demands of pastoral care, Sunday by Sunday preaching and Session meetings.

There were also domestic arrangements to be dealt with. Years before there had been two mission bungalows and a mission hospital, but policies changed and a Government hospital had been built. The civil surgeon advised that the highly trained compounders should be posted to village dispensaries and so spread the medical care. This advice was followed and the expanded medical care has continued to this day. With the mission hospital closed, there was not the same need for the missionary, and with retirement and shifts in policy and the new type of medical work able to be supervised from the Mure Hospital in Nagpur, in time the bungalows were sold.

In the very early days of the mission in Wardha, a church had been built, followed by a large room and, adjoining, another large high-ceilinged room — one room for the medical missionary to consult in and the other for the compounder and his medicines. Then came the policy changes. With the enclosing of the all-round verandahs by trellis to form a study and kitchen and sleeping room — hey presto! — a home for the single missionary and later a manse! Some in the congregation remembered missionary families in bungalows and began to regret the sale of the old ones. However we persuaded them that if we could have the **very latest in** modern conveniences — hardly even being thought of in city mission bungalows at that time — namely a septic tank and toilet, we would find the manse a very satisfactory home!

It was customary for all missionaries, especially before

Wardha shopping centre

the days of electric fans, to sleep outside — always under a
mosquito net. It was an expensive item, but essential to avoid
malaria. We had a small compound (garden area) with a low
wall bordering on the main road. I used to say we were within
spitting distance of the passing cinema-goers! Spitting was
common — and socially acceptable — in those days because of
the habit of chewing betal nuts.

The language study period of two years was on the
whole a peaceful, happy time, with the two "hot weathers"
spent with other new missionaries at the Marathi language
school in the hill station of Mahableshwar near Poona. At the
end of the first spell there, we came down to Poona in the
heat to await the arrival of young Alexander Crawford More.

One of the attractions of the Wardha area was that only
five miles away in the village of Sevagram was the Gandhian
ashram. (When Mahatma Gandhi decided that the salvation
of India must begin in and proceed from "Village India", he
got off the train at Wardha — very near the centre of India
— and walked for five miles into the country. There he sat
down and said "I will make my ashram here", which he did.)

By the time we went to Wardha, the ashram was the well established and extremely active centre of the Gandhian Movement. Gandhi himself had been assassinated in 1948, a sad and dreadful memory for us, for all India and far beyond.

(I had had the great privilege of being taken to meet him during the "Quit India" era. This made my approach to him rather tentative, but he was courteous beyond mere politeness. I was invited to accompany him on his evening walk. We visited some typhoid patients in their homes and he discussed medical questions. Later I joined the congregation sitting on the ground waiting for him to lead the evening prayer.)

In the years of our association with the Gandhian Ashram, the leader was E. A. Aryanaikam with his wife, Asha Devi. We received great friendship there and learned much about simple Indian life. For all of this we found use later when we ourselves decided to live in a village and to live in community there.

In 1949, Margery Sykes came to Sevagram and there began a friendship and a growing common interest which has lasted until today. Margery had come from Shantineketan, near Calcutta, where she had been working with Rabindanath Tagore and had written, with an Indian colleague, a life of C. F. Andrews, missionary and friend of Gandhi. She was then asked to superintend the basic education programme which was planned to fit education more to the needs of rural India, and was taught at Sevagram.

To this basic education programme came graduate and non-graduate teachers, and even directors of education. During our years in Wardha, we had close contact with Sevagram, and George was chaplain to the many Christians who came on the courses. He would cycle out regularly and take services, and he offered English services on Sunday afternoon in our Wardha Church. It was an exciting period for educationalists, with eager argument for and against the basic course.

My memories of the Sunday morning Marathi service in the Wardha Church are very precious. The parishioners were wont to call themselves "Free Church Christians" — presumably from the days before the 1929 Church Union in Scotland. One smiles, remembering, but it is sad evidence of the divisions we brought with the Gospel. Our Church furnishings were very severe, having a platform with a wooden railing for pulpit and a small table in front with a cloth on it. There was a cupboard on each side of the wall behind the pulpit. It is sad to remember the powerful resistance to George's suggestion of a plain curtain being hung along the length of the wall covering the little "kitchen" cupboards. He did manage to get a small cross on the roof above the door that we might witness.

I am deeply moved as I remember these services, especially George's courage and perseverence with the Marathi language. Fortunately there was a book of Common Order, so that he quickly grew familiar with the weekly service. However, he was not so familiar with the Marathi script, and as the climate necessitated that all windows be open, any breeze could quite easily, un-noticed by George, blow a page over – so that, as he said, instead of marrying someone, he might find himself laying them as a foundation stone! I don't think such a calamity ever did happen but it gives an idea of what it meant to take up a 'first charge' in foreign language and conditions!

There was no resident priest in Wardha at that time, but there was a Roman Catholic Church, and we very much enjoyed having the Swedish missionary priest come for a meal on his monthly visits. It was much the same with the Episcopal Church. They had a beautiful little English village-type church with a lovely old-fashioned covered lych gateway in the surrounding wall.

One is amazed now to contemplate the strength of the divisions in Christian missionary activity – all having sheltered under the protection of the British Raj and still continuing in a small district town in the heart of independent, largely Hindu, India. It is a testimony too, to the profound wide tolerance of India and the lack of it in the Christian Church.

The "Mission" had been in our area for many years with very little growth in Christian believers, and George wondered if we could find a new approach for the Gospel in rural India where 80% of the people lived. What about an experiment in living in a village ourselves for a short period as a first move in learning about the people's lives and traditions – a 'blank paper' kind of experiment from which we might be led to a new missionary approach?

This decision was made fairly soon after George began his ministry in the Wardha Church because 'the parish' of the Church included some three hundred villages. George had responsibility for this parish underlined by his current 'hat' of district missionary. It also allowed him to proceed with the training of his (two!) elders in responsibility for leading Church worship. In this he was fairly successful, but not equally so in persuading his Kirk Session to entertain the thought of increasing the number of elders! That had to wait.

Janet and Alex and I used to accompany George in his parish visiting in the two villages where there was a compounder and his dispensary, which we had been asked by the Mission Board in Nagpur to superintend.

One of these villages, Selu, was on the main Nagpur-Wardha road; the other, Allipur, was twenty miles 'into the interior', if I may be allowed to use, for the first and last time, this old colonial expression. We decided that we would choose one of these villages for our experiment.

Selu hadn't a hope from the first. It was within the main-highway and bus reach of all civilised services, whereas Allipur, for the last six miles of the twenty, didn't even have a possible bus road surface, far less a bus to reach any civilisation. Our elderly station wagon could just make it by means of what a friend called George's "circus driving". George was quite clear that the decision would fall on Allipur which, although isolated from civilisation, was the "District Town" holding the weekly market, and undoubtedly, part of rural India. It had no electricity until some thirteen years later, no running water, no sanitation and no qualified doctor.

So it was decided that we would proceed to a ping-pong existence between Wardha and Allipur, beginning cautiously with a few nights in Allipur each month. We were fortunate that a village house, previously used by an evangelist, was available to us. It had one main room and a verandah, and a small room at the side for a kitchen. We slept on the verandha. The walls and floor were made of mud and the verandha had a bamboo trellis. The rafters were of uncut logs. Our beds had wooden frames with string base and our mattresses were of kapok and very thin, as required by the climate.

Later when we were, quite soon, hooked on Allipur, we extended the house by one room and a verandah, and had septic tank sanitation and a brick-based bathing place in the room. We also had accommodation for guests on the verandha. David and Alison Lyon, with a babe and a toddler,

Our Allipur house (with the chimney and three windows!)

were our first guests. Quite an adventure it all was — but it was the beginning, a seed of things to come.

George's energy seemed to spend itself in three areas in the first three years of his missionary life, after language study.

First there was his work as parish minister in Wardha. The parish was about the size of Perthshire, with some three hundred villages, very many of which had not heard the Gospel. There was a compounder with a dispensary in each of two villages and a medical practice extending over a wide area. Parish visiting in these two areas included supervision of the dispensary and a clinic for women specially called on that day. A Communion service was held on these visits, and a few scattered Christian families gathered then. In addition to his ministry in Sevagram, George set out to get to know the Gandhian leaders in the town and the many Gandhian institutions, the civic leaders and the staff of the Government Civil Hospital. Later we were to have a close and very helpful relationship with the hospital which was our first resource in surgical emergency. The mission hospital, the Mure

Memorial, was a further sixty miles away in the city of Nagpur.

The immediate parish work of weekly services, monthly Communion, parish visiting, Sunday School, and Session meetings continued in the Presbyterian way and George's Marathi increased in fluency.

The second area to which George turned his attention in this period was work in the Church Council (the Presbytery). He had two or three spells as Moderator of the Church Council, but would not consider proceeding to the Synod or the General Assembly and its committees, believing at this stage that these posts should be filled by Indian ministers.

Away in the background for many years, the slow, plodding, determined work of the North Indian Church Union Committee had been going on and continued to work towards union — which did not happen for another twenty years or so — but there was urgent and essential work to go on first in the area of handing over finance and institutions from the Mission to the Indian Church. Into the difficult business of this handover George flung himself with all his conviction, information and persuasion. This continued for many years whenever his contribution was requested. He trained his great friend and colleague, Mr. E. Augustine, to undertake all over North India the work of advising Councils and Churches on the legal position, and with much other information for the final transfer of property.

The third subject was one that concerned him greatly from his student days and certainly beyond this Wardha period we are considering just now. That was — how was his call to the ministry of mission to be fulfilled — how was he to find, in the words of the Iona Community collect, "new ways to touch the hearts of men"?

During my first three years in India it was pointed out to me that not all members of the Church of Scotland were missionaries — indeed very few were — so why should we expect all Indian Christians to be missionaries or even missionary-minded? I didn't have an answer to that then and I haven't really got one now, except perhaps to admit that the failure of the local Scottish Church to be 'missionary' is more sad and more culpable than the failure of the Indian Church, and may indeed be contributory. And there is always the possibility that missionary methods — or some of them — were not ideal and best not reproduced anyway. For whatever reason, neither the Church of Scotland locally in Scotland nor the Indian Church in our area was missionary-minded.

At this time of decision about Allipur, David Lyon and George received a cable from George MacLeod (now Very Rev. Lord MacLeod of Fuinary) Leader of the Iona Community — of which they were both members — to the effect that on his fund-raising world tour with Lorna, they could spare us 22 hours. It was typical George MacLeod to do it and as 'out of this world' as usual. It seemed a natural Iona Community occasion while it happened, and not least do I remember his tearing around the Wardha bungalow playing with the children.

For a period of a few years — our first years living in Allipur — we were given the use of a bungalow in Wardha until we were sure we could cope and, fortunately, it was during this time that the MacLeods came. The Lyons were already interested in Allipur and its future and, since the time was short, it was decided that the MacLeods should be brought to Wardha to spend the day and be taken from there the eighteen miles to Allipur.

The visitors arrived in the night and left the next night. One of the men met the plane at Nagpur and drove the MacLeods to Allipur, and the other drove them back the next night, just under seventy miles each way. George and Lorna had some rest, but I think little sleep, in our 22 hours.

George, Lorna, David, George and I went to Allipur in the Land Rover, acquired by the mission in Scotland, while Alison looked after the children. Even now it is difficult to look at Allipur through their eyes. Since my first spell in India, I had been used to visiting village dispensaries and George, easily integrating anywhere, felt nothing was strange. Certainly George MacLeod could give us an unbiased opinion and he was quite clear — "No way attempt to stay in Allipur. Much better choose Selu on the main highway". Despite this advice, we were inexpressively appreciative of his visit. I can't think of anyone but George MacLeod who would have tackled it and he did it for us. Now, even as then, I feel amazed and proud to remember he was there — and Lorna with him.

As we proceeded round the village, Lorna was a tremendous success with her untiring interest in everything and in the crowding, awed children. The crowning magic was her instant camera out of which popped the instant photographs! Then back to Wardha, a meal, and off to

Nagpur Airport for a plane leaving about midnight. It didn't seem true then and it doesn't seem true now — just wonderful!

Medical Work

Before the present-day medical knowledge of the cause, prevention and treatment of the diseases that killed the missionaries, wives and children — whose names appear on church gravestones up and down India — it was quite out of the question for a missionary to take his family to live in an Indian village. It would have been regarded as completely irresponsible. This security had been fairly recently won and was the operative signal for us to go.

Allipur and the surrounding villages were fortunate to have had the services of our trained compounder and the village 'doctors', who were primary school teachers and shopkeepers. Their medical qualifications consisted of being able to read the instructions (in English) on the packets and bottles of medicines easily available over the counter in the town. With a little bit of luck in diagnosis they saved many lives. So also did the Aruvedic (Indian medicine) practitioners, but there was no one able to care especially for women. (The average strictures in Purdha observance applied not only to obstetrics and gynaecology but also to abdominal and chest conditions. The doctor would sit outside the mud house and receive shouted answers about the patient's condition and advise and prescribe on the information given.)

There had always been locally trained village midwives — the training being handed on from mother to daughter in one of the outcaste groups — and women medical missionaries in the early days made a great effort to give them a simple training, especially in hygiene.

We didn't have, in our day, the huge cholera epidemics of the past. Much had been done in the prevention of cholera by innoculation and chlorination of drinking water but we still had the occasional outbreak. At the first rumour of a case of cholera, the Government innoculation routine went into action. Passengers in buses arriving at a town anywhere near a cholera outbreak were liable to find themselves driven into the hospital compound and innoculated without even a 'by your leave'. For chlorination, it was uncertain merely to put a quantity of chlorine powder into the well as, by constant dilution, the effect was diminished. I can picture

George sitting under a tree by the nearest well pouring measures of the powder into each water container as the water was drawn up. The effect was more certain that way and he trained the people in the procedure. The chlorination was accompanied by advice to boil all drinking water, especially for children. For ourselves, we boiled our drinking water for 30 years — and attributed our excellent health to this discipline (that and sleeping under mosquito nets to prevent malaria).

It happened that on our first few days' stay in our village house — the timing carefully chosen in the safe month of September, rains and epidemics having finished for the year — we were faced with a small residual cholera episode. What were we to do? Retreat with the children back to Wardha or even to Nagpur seemed reasonable, but we had felt so sure we were to be **here**, children and all. So we thought and prayed and stayed.

Our cholera case routine was simple. When told of a suspected case, we visited and gave an injection of the then very new psychiatric drug, Largactol. This use was entirely our own discovery. We tried it because the reports said it was a superb sedative. In addition to its use for mental illness, it was muscle-relaxing and stopped vomiting. This last was what first made us try it, because if you can get simple sulphanilamide tablets to remain in the stomach, you're there, because the simplest sulpha-drug is very efficient in curing the cholera and allowing drinking water to cope with the dehydration. The sedation and relaxing effects eased first the distress and secondly relieved the very painful cramps.

In the meantime our intravenous syringe had been boiling up at home, and we collected it and a couple of bottles of saline before returning to the fray. The medical work was 'combined operations' for us, always. George would tie the saline bottle to the rafters and control the flow, while I kneeled on the mud floor to insert the needle. Collapsed veins are not the easiest to get into, but with a primitive tournique, we made it most times.

The decision was made that George would open and manage a clinic for women and children and also manage a fairly comprehensive pharmacy, while I would doctor in the clinic. This medical work became our principal daily service for four days a week plus one concurrent day, market day. George ran the leprosy clinic.

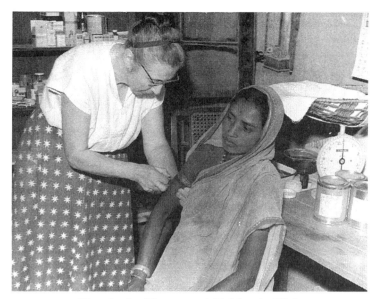

Mary in the Women and Children's Clinic

Leprosy is a serious scourge in India and was from the earliest medical missionary days a challenge and a cause of deep concern. No effective treatment was available until some twenty years ago. Many different treatments had been tried, and in many countries complete separation from the community was insisted upon. So unproductive were the efforts to effect a cure of leprosy that the medical profession became discouraged and serious research was not carried out. However there were always places where leprosy patients were cared for, and doctors and nurses gave their lives to that care. Eventually, out of this continuing care, research did recommence. During the enthusiastic research for ever new drugs to treat tuberculosis, one was found, inadvertantly, to effect the beginnings of cure for leprosy in a patient suffering from both diseases! Now leprosy research is an accepted part of medical science.

Like the Christian missionaries, the followers of Gandhi were concerned to care for leprosy patients. Manohar Divan, a member of Gandhi's Ashram, went from there to superintend a leprosy sanitorium and agricultural community five miles from Wardha. It is of interest that on Gandhi's advice his first move, before beginning the work on the ground, was to visit many Christian missionary leprosy institutions of which

George in first Leprosy Clinic on verandha of our first Allipur home

there were a number in India. Later the Gandhi Memorial
Leprosy Foundation was established, and it was by the doctor
in charge of the Foundation that we were challenged to take
seriously the treatment of leprosy as a part of our Allipur
work. When I hedged, saying we didn't get much experience
of leprosy in the Western Infirmary in Glasgow, he said: "We
will train you". We were humbled by his final plea – "You
people," he said, "are living in a village, and we don't have
any trained workers in villages yet." They had a leprosy
treatment centre near Sevagram and George went there for
training.

Both the women and children's clinic and the leprosy
clinic work were all done in outdoor patient clinics – the
women's clinic was open for four days a week, but the leprosy
clinic was open only on the market day.

Our leprosy work began with two orange boxes in a
grass shelter under a tree, and on the first day we had its
presence announced by the village 'Town Crier'. He went
round the village banging a drum and calling "Brothers and
sisters today there is a medicine place for treating skin

conditions" (we used this euphemism for the leprosy work). We had three patients that day and finished up with around 1,700 on the records.

The routine leprosy treatment consisted of daily tablets, and patients came latterly from several hundred villages. Once the treatment was established, one man could come from a village on behalf of several patients. We would collect all the medicines in their individual packets, each tied up in a spare piece of his dhoti – several yards of cotton material wound most skilfully into baggy trousers. Illiteracy certainly does not mean a lack of intelligence, and it is often accompanied by an extraordinary memory, so that one could be confident that each little packet would reach its rightful owner.

When the rains came, our little shelter got washed away, and we moved over to the verandah of our home which had a corrugated iron roof. This house and verandah later became the clinic itself. Eventually, with very welcome 'War-on-Want' money, we had a custom-built leprosy clinic with a large room for patients to wait and collect their routine tablets.

George, Mary and Rev. Manohar Londhe on step of new Leprosy Clinic

There was a smaller room, peaceful and intimate. Here George met with new patients and dealt with any problems in the routine patients. This part of his leprosy work was indeed a ministry. Leprosy in a spouse is a reason for divorce in

33

India, and George was concerned to persuade families against this tragic move. He pointed out the tremendous advance in treatment. I believe his quiet assurance and obvious sincerity and concern moved many families away from the break.

On one occasion George was accosted by a young farmer friend whom he had got to know in the process of providing his well with a diesel pump. This young man had had to undertake the responsibility of head of the family on his father's death when he himself was not yet thirty. These responsibilities were great, especially with a young sister's marriage to arrange as well as the joint family concerns to attend to. In addition he was a member of the Gram Panchayat — the group of five men who constituted the local village governing body.

When George saw him, the young farmer was apparently in the stage of hypo-mania of a manic-depressive illness. He had refused to go to hospital in Nagpur nearly 80 miles away and his family and friends were losing control of the situation. They had had recourse to tying him up on occasions, and he had come personally to George.

George and I had had interest in psychiatric illness thrust upon us by the occasional occurence of psychotic episodes amongst young men in the village. We had been able to cope because of the literature at that time about the development of new pschiatric drugs and their recent availability in India. Also, in the clinic we had had several young women suffering from post-natal depression, which we had treated with some success.

Having convinced himself that there was no hope of passing the buck and getting professional psychiatric care for him in the city, George asked him if he would take medicine from us. We started with our great standby, largactol, and were much alarmed when it was reported (fortunately quite soon) that he was taking one himself and handing them round to his wife and family! So we retrieved the tablets and started again, realising that out-patient treatment was liable to be hazardous.

Fortunately the conference buildings were empty at this point and we established our patient with his wife and two children **and** his grandmother and grandfather in one of the two conference houses. They settled in happily and the patient came up the few yards to our house for his tablet medication; while he remained in his hypo-manic state, he spent many hours in continued talk with George so that we had to upgrade his sedation. When we decided an injection was called for, he refused to have it unless his wife had one too — so we had to explain to her and persuade her that a Vitamin 'B' injection would not harm her!

At one point there was an entertainment in the village and we thought it better he should not attend. George engaged him in conversation until midnight, when he took his departure down to the fair and eventually climbed on to the roof of a bus and fell asleep! It was quite an exhausting and nerve-racking experience but eventually, after weeks, he responded to treatment and did not have a recurrence while we were in Allipur.

There was one very interesting aspect about this episode. During the very excitable period of his illness he became very caring and outgoing. He proceeded to bring us all the mentally disturbed people he could find, and thus established us — that is George, with his patience and caring and very good Marathi, and me to the background to pore over the books with him in medical decisions — in the field of mental health care.

Without specific training we went cannily. There was much manic depressive illness. We recognised schizophrenia, and had the appropriate medication available, though that was a long business and patients came and went. The comment was often made that it was surprising to have depressive illness in a peaceful, rural situation, but in fact the rapid social change in the cities did have its effect in the rural situation. The beginnings of the break-up of joint families' system, the advent of electricity and irrigation and new types of seeds and routines in a centuries-old farming system, combined with anxiety about literacy, meant that there was an increase in mental distress.

For most of the 22 years in Allipur our work was based in the clinic. In our very early tentative period we did respond to calls for medical help in surrounding and even quite distant villages. We discontinued this on several grounds —

It was very time consuming; only the wealthy and important tended to call us — and there was little time to see a few of the needy crowds; the normal midwifery cases tended to be completed before we arrived, and the majority of the serious ones required to be packed into the Land Rover and taken to hospital.

35

So we decided the best economy of time and skill was for us to remain in the central village where people came weekly to the bazaar. The very sick could be carried in a turned-up bed, to be examined in the comparatively sterile conditions of our clinic hut, kept there for supervision or sent on by Land Rover to the Government hospital 20 miles away. By this system in the end we served some 400 villages.

Remuneration

One necessary activity which fell to George's lot was to sit at the seat of custom. Perhaps I should describe what we actually did in this matter and then try to describe what our aim was. In this, as in much else, we followed the Gandhian example; we offered our skills and services free, asking that all necessary accommodation and medicines be supplied by the people of the village. To make this possible we used the cheapest effective medicines from Indian pharmaceutical companies (keeping, of course, a check on effectiveness). They were amazingly cheap in comparison with imported drugs, or the products of the Western companies with factories in India.

However, there were costly necessary exceptions to this rule. One very important one was cortisone, the only effective treatment to save sight in eyes affected by leprosy – and often, again to save sight, injections of Vitamin A. There were many patients who could not pay. We were able to subsidise these costs from contributions, often from Women's Guilds, both Indian and Scottish, and by special pleading in the case of anti-tetanus innoculation to cover mothers and babes.

We used all methods occurring to us to carry out a healing ministry. One little illustration might put the minds and hearts of readers at ease about whether or not it is justifiable, or caring, to expect Indian villagers to pay for medicines – and even worse, a "consultation fee" was indeed paid as our policy of self-support-rural-medicine developed.

Latterly, patients came from some 400 villages around Allipur, from up to at least 20 miles distance. So that they wouldn't be returning the next week, I was anxious that, if possible, they would take four weeks medicine. This was necessary to combat long-standing deficiencies – acute conditions were treated there and then by injection and some 5 day capsules. Hiraman kept George right about real poverty, and when there was an outcry about inability to pay,

George would begin to undo the packet of medicines (a newspaper packet) and say "Well, I'll give you two weeks medicine". Before he could suggest they send for the other half, there would be greater protestations and large denomination roupee notes would be produced! After a few repeats of this programme our own minds and hearts were put at ease. (We know the clinic still goes on, thanks to an Order of South Indian Roman Catholic nuns with a Belgian Missionary Mother in charge, who took over from us. One of these nuns is a nursing sister and we have just recently learned three of them live in our little house — lovely! We rather expect their methods will be similar to ours, but our aim was that by our experimenting, it would be seen to be possible for general practitioners to live in Indian villages and make a satisfactory living by charging according to ability to pay. They would be more aware than we could be of patients' circumstances and probably more able than I felt I was to organise into their day the more remunerative home visits.)

Teaching

George's familiarity with the Marathi language also allowed him to undertake a considerable amount of teaching on medical matters as well as the biblical teaching and discussion that developed from Hiraman's instructions for Baptism. George's lay teaching in our medical work concerned innoculations, diet, family planning, ante-natal care, and preventive medicine. Innoculations-teaching included anti-tetanus work which covered both mother and child but which we introduced because of the alarming number of lovely healthy babies who died of untreatable tetanus before the age of 8 days. We found some people, notably school teachers, who were interested in the more sophisticated 'triple innoculations' against diptheria, whooping cough and tetanus. When we began our clinic, the government had already undertaken general smallpox vaccinations (though we still saw many cases — on social visits the baby might be produced to show off how many pox he had). In our last years, all children born in hospital had B. C. G. innoculations against tuberculosis and there were some B. C. G. touring teams as well as those vaccinating against smallpox.

There was constant teaching about water-borne disease in the clinic and the danger of pools of water with their malaria-bearing; also about the prevention of night-blindness by eating Vitamin A-rich yellow vegetables and fruit. The medical treatment of this condition sometimes had the appearance of magic. A child with long-standing night-blindness brought from a distance, receiving an injection of Vitamin A, would begin to see as the dark fell when they reached home.

A lot of time was spent teaching about diet. Many patients were vegetarians by religious teaching or because they couldn't afford to buy meat, so it was essential that they realised the importance of eating lentils to provide second-class protein and iron, and green vegetables for iron and vitamins.

Pregnant women often suffered from severe anaemia and vitamin deficiency, although they would have remained fairly fit if they had eaten all the food that was available for them. However, their response to any deficiency or debility was to cut down on one necessary item of food after another, from a traditional teaching based originally on religious sanctions, until they might end up eating only rice.

All such teaching had to be repeated constantly, and it was most effective in George's well understood Marathi (though I made my contribution in my broad-Glasgow-type acquired Marathi!). Throughout, we kept up to date with the medical literature, especially in rural and children's medical care.

Later in our time in Allipur, the General Nursing Council of India introduced a new scheme as part of the general nursing training whereby student nurses, in small groups, would spend some days in a village. They were to look after themselves, experiencing village conditions for themselves, and making house-to-house visitations in order to learn about village life.

This was a very pleasant scheme for us and we had happy evening discussions on a wide variety of subjects. Electricity had been installed by the time this programme had been established in Allipur, and in support of my aim of making village domestic life as easy and attractive as possible to tempt professional families to settle in a village, we had installed a good electric lighting system in our house with a fridge, an electric iron and kettle and fans. Gleefully I would lead the conversation on until invariably someone would ask: "Did you bring these from the U. K. or are they American?" Then I would announce: "All our household equipment, and all the machinery in the workshop, is made in India". The girls were really surprised, and this provided the opening for George to hold forth on India's rapid and wide development, its growing export trade, its development of nuclear power and manufacture of railway engines and aeroplanes, etc. etc. Although we spent our working life in rural India, George was deeply interested in all and every evidence of both rural and urban development in India. He was ever anxious to develop the people's self esteem and eradicate any residual post-colonial feelings.

Hiraman

Hiraman became a great friend and filled a big place in our life. The wealthy farmer who had provided our first little clinic room was himself a leprosy patient and cared for leprosy patients when he could. Once, after a brief absence, we returned to find Hiraman established in an empty room opening on to the same verandah as our clinic room did, and we found he was a leprosy patient! You can imagine what public health authorities in the United Kingdom would think of a leprosy patient sitting in the child welfare clinic waiting room!

Hiraman had been discharged from the leprosarium where he had been treated for some years, discharged as a "burnt-out" case and certified as non-infectious – so that both he and the authorities had been concerned and careful. We further discovered that he did not belong to this village (he had indeed been disowned by his family, and his wife had returned to her family), and on his discharge he had to choose where to go and remake his life. He had in fact chosen Allipur because he had heard that there were missionaries there, and he thought he would be cared for if need arose. He had marked deformity of his hands and feet and no sensation in his limbs because of the destruction of nerves by the disease. This meant that he could sustain quite severe injury without being aware of it. This did indeed happen and he became very ill.

When we examined him, he kept his feet under his blanket, and finding he had a high fever, we sought the reason in his chest, throat and abdomen. Finding no cause we decided, as one does in tropical medicine practice, that he probably had typhoid – but he did not respond well to anti-typhoid tablets. He at last revealed his damaged foot with toes affected and the wound filled with maggots. (Please don't feel horror at this — maggots are excellent cleaners of wounds!) I fetched a basin of disinfectant and forceps; but it is George I have a picture of, on his knees on the mud verandah, picking up maggots one by one and dropping them into the basin. There is an instinctive fear of leprosy in most people and we too had it but, until then, the leprosy treatment we had been called upon to do had been the handing out of pills. Now, having faced the maggots, we experienced being close to what leprosy could do to a human being, and in coping with it, the strange unreasoning fear left us completely.

By the time Hiraman had recovered and returned to his tailoring we had decided that we would have to divide our resources on Market Day — George going to the leprosy clinic and I to the women and children's clinic. (Later we were able to train a village woman to be in the clinic, explaining the arrangements and helping as she could). In these earlier days the crowding and demanding of the waiting women — and my poor command of Marathi — nearly drove me to despair. Hiraman, working at his sewing machine — his new mended feet able to return to the foot pedal — saw my confusion and one evening he came to us and offered to help by organising the patients. He would find those seriously ill or furthermost distant, who might need to be attended out of turn, and would settle disputes. But his most lasting contribution was to suggest a system of giving patients daily numbers, to which I added more permanent numbers made of cut-up cardboard toothpaste and shaving cream containers for their own number in our records. It was always a surprise to me that they managed, without pockets, or handbags, to bring them. That was nothing to their surprise that, coming after a period of years, I was able to tell them all their family history and medical past!

Hiraman remained in Allipur for some years, continuing with his help in the clinic and developing his "Ready Made Childrens' Clothes" business. Even we, as a family, after the long accepted "rule" of the durzis (Tailors), found it surprising and exciting!

However we returned from a furlough absence to find Hiraman gone. We were sad and puzzled, but in due course he returned to visit us with the tale of a community of leprosy people who had gradually collected near a hospital in a town in the North of India. The place was chosen so that

Hiraman and SupiBai

medical aid was at hand if required. We never got to see it but it sounded a most remarkable happening. All kinds of religions, tribes and castes seemed to be drawn, and a very real fellowship formed on the basis of common misfortune. Hiraman had found acceptance there.

He came every summer to visit us, and eventually announced that he had remarried and wanted to bring his wife, SupiBai, for George to baptize. George had questioned Hiraman eagerly about all the circumstances of this new life he was leading and had learned that there was a Roman Catholic church or mission near the community. He was anxious that Hiraman would get involved in the local Christian community and life, but Hiraman had set his heart on SupiBai being baptised by George, as he himself had been.

So it came about that the last supremely significant and memorable occasion that took place in Allipur before we left — actually in the clinic building, our first mud home, by Hiraman's special wish in the "Office" room where he himself had been brought to an experience of Jesus' love and salvation **and** had often witnessed to it — was SupiBai's baptism.

41

Surgical Camp

Not long after the completion and opening of the Allipur High School, George was approached by some of the surgeons at Sevagram's new medical college about the possibility of having a surgical camp in Allipur. This was indeed an exciting prospect, and entailed much organisation in the village. This was again made possible as a joint-community project by George's bringing them and holding them together under the Christian umbrella.

There was plenty of scope for such a camp as it turned out — hernias and tonsils and gynaecological surgery, etc. etc., as well as arrangements for a future eye camp. A widely representative committee was formed and a door-to-door collection was made to help with expenses. The school was willingly made available and staff and servants co-operated.

Three classrooms began as theatres, but as the hall and other classrooms filled up with post-operative patients, the three operation tables were moved into one classroom. It was an impressive sight — the electricians from the medical college hospital fitted up the central light over each table, and one long instrument table was supervised by a very competant South Indian Sister.

The hospital staff members lived in our community conference accommodation and there was a very happy fellowship in the evenings. We felt they were fairly comfortably introduced to village life and the possibilities of village medicine.

I will round off this section with two "snapshots" of George's own peculiar and precious contributions to the Allipur medical work. It delights me to recall them.

After some years of ex-army khaki shorts and shirts — the tail worn inside or out according to the climate and the social occasion — George began to wear the Indian outfit of pyjama and kurta. (Pyjama is an Indian word adapted into English by the pre-independence soldiers who spent so many years in India. Pyjama is not necessarily night wear — it is full dress and very wide, and the shirt [kurta] is wide, too, with long sleeves and a buttoned-up round neck). George found it very comfortable wear in the Indian climate; his were made of white khadi (homespun and hand-woven cotton material). This sartorial move was very much appreciated by our village friends. I confess I didn't follow him in this because, although I loved to wear a sari on special occasions, it was not so comfortable, consisting as it does of at least six yards of material gathered round the waist and over the shoulder. It required an ankle-length petticoat, with a blouse also tucked in! I wore a full, ballet-length khadi-material skirt and a cool white blouse. (George, if he read this, would raise his eyebrows and say: "Well, there are two lengths of ballet skirt". I know he would because I heard him once! That was the quickness and the dearness of his humour, which I am finding so hard to catch in order to recount it).

The medical contribution of the outfit was that the flowing material in legs and sleeves seemed to encourage George in the dance routines he was fond of using to entertain children. He developed the routines into a therapy for depressive illness, and for use in dealing with illness in general, and it was very often effective – indeed practically irresistible! For children, he had an elephant dance routine which later became familiar in Glasgow and Iona.

George's remarkable patience often made him the only one who could persuade a reluctant infant to suck from a bottle. Normally, bottle feeding was not encouraged – our concern was more with the introduction of supplementary food while the infant continued to breast feed. The question of weaning, as we know it, never came up, for that would mean the end of all milk, probably the only protein for the child. If buying milk for an under-nourished child was suggested, the question was usually asked "For how many days will we give this milk?" Milk was unknown to them as children's food and when, by any mischance, breast milk became unavailable, efforts to feed the child rice water by spoon were usually a failure. We introduced feeding bottles – though with misgivings because of the difficulty of hygiene – but none of us had any success in getting the idea over. It was here that George's patience and his profound caring had been known to succeed. This whole exercise did not occur very often, but it caused a memorable sensation.

Water

Against the background of the daily routine, George's fertile brain was turning out idea after idea in response to the needs of the situation. An outstanding need was for easier access to water. The statistics about how many women members in each joint family were required to spend most of each day carrying water after drawing it from the well were quite staggering.

Over the years one learns how a life partner ticks — and some people tick much more quietly than others! I learned that George's fertile brain ticked **very** quietly and had been long active before the first signs appeared of highly planned activity. The first sign apparent to me of plumbing ahead was to find him sitting outside in the warm quiet evening with a supported wheel of some sort before him which he meditatively turned to right and left, staring into the far distance the while. In fact he was threading water pipes with a tool called a hand-die.

The period of the latrine-pit was short, mercifully, and we got a septic tank, George having learned "how" when one was put in the Wardha manse. But strangely enough, septic tanks are like washing machines — they can be plumbed-in or hand flushed! I see the parallel is not complete because nobody ever had an electric washing machine who didn't have access to running water for a hose — but you see the point. The difference, of course, between a plumbed-in septic tank and a not plumbed one was more basic than in the case of the washing machine and to get oneself a plumbed-in septic tank where there was no running water because of no pipes, called for considerable brain fertility and determination.

Farming

Village farmers were employed to farm, of course, but George discussed with them all the new questions of irrigation, fertilization, new kinds of seeds and marketing. The biggest adventure was augmenting the few orange trees already in the 'field' we had bought till we had quite a notable orchard. We also ventured into dairy farming — i.e. three buffaloes with a calf quite soon, also some poultry.

Our farming was basically tenant farming, with continuing interest in modernisation. The attempt at dairy farming — which involved a hope of co-operatively selling milk in Wardha where the demand was high — was exciting but not a great success. A Lambretta three wheeled motor cycle was purchased for the milk delivery. George took and passed his driving test, and had us all learning with varying success! But the exceedingly bad road for 18 miles with pot-holes of all sizes resulted in butter rather than milk arriving at the town! It was worth a trial, but eventually the

Fruit growing experiment – first class Nagpur oranges

decision went against it and our Lambretta was sold into the rickshaw business.

We much enjoyed having poultry, but it, too, was not a tremendous commercial success and suffered a lot from the onslaught of mongoose; but we continued the tenant farming and were closely interested also in the development of market gardening made possible by irrigation. George was very interested in the plans for nearer facilities for selling cotton, which was the cash crop in this part of India. The growing of wheat was introduced in our time and gradually began to take the place of Jawar – the local maize.

With the help of War on Want, George had an exciting venture into land reform. He was able to buy a few acres of land, which in turn he was able to hand out to a landless peasant to manage and cultivate and gradually pay up the cost. He accomplished this while we were still there – and great was the joy of it!

Electricity

Gandhi had said he would not have electricity in his house until it had been supplied to every village in India. We were not so altruistic! We awaited the arrival of the poles and wire drums in Allipur with selfish excitement. For years we had watched the poles being first dumped and then raised, all

45

the way from Wardha. Every time a new lot appeared we wonderd aloud if this lot would be for Allipur. It seemed an endless wait.

But, in the meantime, preparations were being made by George in Allipur. In order that he might begin teaching the basics, he purchased a generator and set to with the principles, so that when at last the great day came, no time was lost. It should be understood that electricity was spreading through the length and breadth of rural India — but not for house lighting. Certainly tube lighting in the village streets, but the main business was agriculture — pumps in the wells. What specially enthused me was to see both pupils and further-studying teachers out in the dusty streets under the street lighting, studying. The eagerness for education was a joy to see. It was not poor electricity supply that prevented house-wiring. Nobody in an Indian village except the farm owners and missionaries could afford the cost of electricity, let alone the installing cost.

Failing to get any wire men from Wardha, George proceeded to wire our own house for practise and teaching purposes. All wires had to be enclosed in a wooden casing. He put in all kinds of wiring and switches for teaching — both light and power. As in all missionary houses, a fridge was put in to preserve the medicaments, but usually the complaint was that you couldn't get at them for the butter! We had been in the habit of eating our evening meal outside in the coolness. We didn't change this immediately (or at all, for it was lovely) because when the power was switched on at long last in Allipur, it was supplied only on alternate days!! We had a motor-powered fridge and the first indication that the power had returned was the sound of the fridge motor!

Scottish War on Want folk, when they heard we were living in an Indian village, wrote to offer money. But, apart from the repair of damaged wells, and the building of one or two, George didn't want any money just then. He didn't want the imperialist situation of having money — just yet! He continued with his electrical teaching, his supplying of pumps and their repair and mechanical workshop skills. The books were available in both Marathi and English. Then he wrote to War on Want and said "I'm ready — Give". They gave him all that he needed for his workshop, which he housed in the now disused farm shed — a 2 ton lathe, a hack saw, electric and gas welding equipment, a pillar drill, hand tools for the

46

bench, steel cupboards and much more of which I am ignorant.

George had read it and understood it and knew it with his head, but there was still the proving of it! His description of his first welding action was very vivid. He had read about it often, the book was there; but he still had to put on his protective goggles, tell the apprentice lads to stand back — read again what he was to do — then **do** it! and it worked!! We worked together on the medical work Monday to Thursday, but once the workshop was operative, I saw very little of him Friday to Sunday!

I don't think he had perhaps more than five or six apprentices all together, because there was no work for them. The workshops were all in the towns. George's most apt and rewarding apprentice was a village blacksmith's son. (It was with him that the whole set-up was left when we returned to Scotland. He paid what he could and George was warned that

At work on the lathe

47

he, Madhu, would sell it all as soon as we had left Allipur. But not so. The workshop is still going strong, employing three men as well as Madhu himself. Now the road to the village is a bus road with a bypass round the village, and there is a good deal of work in bus repairs).

India has known changes in decades that took centuries in the West. One story

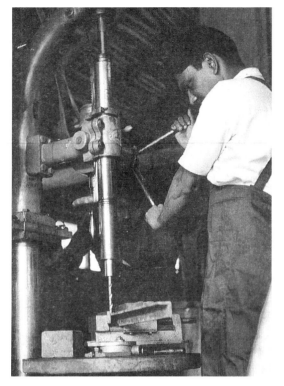

Pillar drill

illustrates this. Three very adventuresome village men — two carpenters I think, the other with more mechanical skill — had got together all the pieces of a saw-mill except the motor and the electrification, and at this point came to George for help.

George was able to get the necessary motor. He had done the electrification, and experienced one more period of apprehension as he stood by this huge, lethal, cutting machine and switched it on — it was O.K. Some time later he was called to see some hitch. There was a crowd round the saw-mill — there usually was — and out of it came a little figure, not very steady on his legs, perhaps four years old. He announced, "ek phase zala" — "one phase is gone"! I had a sudden realisation that a whole generation will grow up not unfamiliar with electricity and its wonders!

High School

For many years free Government primary education had been available in Indian villages for boys and girls (though girls would always be less likely to be able to attend regularly because of the domestic work expected of them). There were also some middle school classes. In our area there was a Hindu Yeshwant Rural Education Society which aimed to put a high school in as many villages as possible, along with the occasional college.

Unlike our attitude in the West, where a building is a first requirement for a school, they had already some hundreds of high school scholars from surrounding villages (those farthest away living in lodgings in Allipur) studying in the Temple guest house, in the Government school building after school hours, under trees etc. The Government was all ready to build their school, but they must provide the land on which it would be built – and no land was available, and no one would offer land.

At this time our workshop was situated in the community compound and, again with War on Want money, George had bought a piece of land in an excellent position for the workshop. It was not difficult for the community members to decide that the school's need was greater than the workshop's and the land was offered to the authorities concerned with the school.

However, there were problems arising from there being different religious communities in the village – Hindu, Muslim and Sikh. This offer of land galvanized them all into wanting each community to have its own high school – and there was deadlock because it was not possible for them to meet together and discuss. In our time in Allipur there had been several such stalemates and in this situation it had always proved possible for George to offer a Christian venue in which they all could meet without breaking any taboos. They met in this way on George's invitation and, with his quiet persuasive skill, he convinced them that Allipur could not accommodate more than one high school and that it would be quite possible for the three religious communities to support the one school. This was something of a triumph. (The school thrives till this day with a multi-religious staff).

The War on Want land was handed over with great ceremony and gratitude as it was the one necessary enabling

Yeshwant High School, Allipur

circumstance to open the Government coffers. From then, George was held in great esteem far beyond the material value of the gift – any credit rightly due to War on Want brushed aside! – and, in due course, the completed building (plus a further War on Want gift in the form of a well) was opened by the Governor of Maharashtra State in person – George and I both being on the platform!

Banking

As the Indian Government became more aware of the needs of the rural three quarters of the country, the State Bank of India managers in the district towns began to receive instructions to set about arranging for sub branches of the bank to be introduced in the larger villages. George first heard of this through his Wardha bank manager rather tentatively enquiring about the car-worthiness of the road to Allipur.

In the end the manager came along and met a group of people George had thought might make use of a branch of the State Bank in the village. A building was eventually found for "The State Bank of India, Allipur Branch" and, after suitable preparation, was opened with some few words by George with, on the platform, the Wardha bank manager and the new young manager of the Allipur Branch!

This was a real advance and help in the village development; but of course a bank is a bank is a bank, and it just can't work without security – and security was just what most of the local small farmers did not have. They did, however, need loans to buy seeds at seed-time, to be returned at harvest, hopefully. Money lenders were willing to lend, but

George on 'Banking' before officially opening the Allipur State Bank branch

their interest was exorbitant, and so George wondered about a co-operative bank. He began one with one thousand rupees of War on Want money.

This venture called for much patient teaching. At first the teaching was not heeded and the loans were looked on as hand-outs until all the capital was handed out and more was requested. To such expectant borrowers George patiently explained the system, pointing out that there was no more money nor would there be until their pals had returned their loans. That penny dropped quite quickly, and the word went round about the working of a co-operative bank. The bank began to work, and a low interest rate was introduced. When we came to leave India the Bank's capital had doubled.

For many years George had worked on the Presbytery Finance Committee, which greatly benefitted from his accountancy skill. He also taught double entry book-keeping to the Mure Hospital Bursar — Karim David — who later left that work to develop a piece of urban development work.

51

Over the years in Allipur, George's training in accountancy, which might have seemed a waste of time, was used by God for the loving of our neighbour.

Driving

We had a colleague, Dr. Peggy Martin, who also had a village clinic on the other side of Nagpur. She had been Medical Superintndent in the Mure Hospital in Nagpur for most of her service, but she saw that it was time to step down and let an Indian lady doctor take her place. At that point she developed the dispensary building to make a small home for herself. She made a tremendous contribution to the health of women and children in that area.

Realising that she was the only driver in the village, she decided it would be better for someone else to be able to drive in an emergency. She gave her compounder a fortnight's holiday and sent him to George in Allipur to be taught to drive.

I offer this one example of many lads who were sent to George, more usually to have him put the finishing touches before the final driving test. When we decided that we did not any longer need a driver and general factotum, since we both drove, George trained our all-purpose man to drive large vehicles and got him through that test to give him a further qualification. George always seemed to be teaching someone driving skills in his spare time!

Allipur Community

For six years we had in Allipur a resident community, an experiment born out of a desire to share the concept of community experienced by George and his missionary colleague and friend, David Lyon, through their membership of the Iona Community.

While the Allipur Community worked out its life and plans in the tropical heat and rain and pleasant cool winters of India, its roots were in the green island of Iona and the Community born there. Their common roots were in the Gospel of Jesus. The Iona Community was conceived out of the pain of the economic inequality of Govan in the 1930's, in the general depression of that time; the Allipur Community was conceived out of the pain of economic inequality in the Nagpur Church Council. The inequality was between members of the Church Council, equal before God and in

Allipur Community minus Scottish adults and some children

their service of the Church, i.e. between Indian ordained ministers and foreign missionary ordained ministers; all this within the pervasive poverty of India.

I think the question of unshared poverty, of privilege and affluence, was always very near the surface of George's thinking and conscience. When he decided to go to Allipur to live and share what he could of his privilege in education and training **and** the Gospel salvation won for all by Jesus, he felt he was inevitably scratching the surface but also that he was called to "scratch" in the meantime! He scratched away cheerfully and most usefully and, above all, lovingly. As it turned out in the end, the one thing that seemed to have got through was his message about Jesus.

Two threads of personal friendship running through George's life came together and wove a pattern for the six years of the Allipur Community. These were David Lyon and Manohar Londhe. David's first coming together with George could have looked like only the merest chance and passing encounter. During the 1939-45 war both men were stationed in Orkney on different islands — David in Kirkwall brought a team of his Highland Regiment soldiers to play a game of

Allipur Community Leaders — George More, Manohar Lhonde and David
Lyon, who had been leading the Sunday morning service

football with a team of George's gunners. They met for a
friendly chat in the Mess and parted at the end of the game.

David and George came face to face some three years
later in St. Mary's College, St. Andrews. In those unspeakably
peaceful two years, friendship and faith grew together; then
George graduated, was ordained as a missionary and we left
for India.

The thread seemed broken. David continued his course,
he and Alison met and grew together. He finished his course
and Alison and he became engaged to be married. After a year
at Union Seminary, New York, they were married. David took
up the work of Student Christian Movement Secretary in
Glasgow and that seemed to be that. However, after some
years there came David's letter — "We feel called to be
missionaries and have asked to be sent to Nagpur" —
wonderful news!

In the next years the community idea took root and
flourished. Our first two years in India were spent in Nagpur
in half of a mission bungalow, as already recounted. Against
the back wall of these large mission compounds there was
usually a row of small houses — originally built as servants'
quarters. In the older days, missionaries usually had several
servants and people welcomed this work. However
missionaries got used to fewer servants, and the houses

54

became available for families needing accommodation. In one of these houses in our compound lived a young man and his wife, Manohar and Ruby Londhe, and their children. He was an evangelist between jobs and a primary teacher meantime.

Once George was introduced to this young man, their friendship began; but soon we were off to Language School. When we returned with two of a family, the Londhe family had gone — he posted somewhere as an evangelist. But soon after George was called to the Wardha Church, Manohar was appointed as his assistant. He was stationed in Hingaonghat, where George had care of a new church, and later Manohar was ordained, by which time we had moved full-time into Allipur. George maintained a close friendship with Manohar and Ruby and shared his thoughts on mission and community, until eventually, the three men were hot on the trail of a community in Allipur.

It was not easy to make clear to the church authorities in India and Scotland what they wanted to do. In the event, these bodies showed a great deal of trust in view of the outlandish-seeming plan. Permission was given to finance the buying of a field close to the village and to build the necessary small houses, by the sale of the mission bungalow that had been provided for the Mores as a temporary measure. This was the Church of Scotland's financial contribution. The Nagpur Church Council released Manohar from his charge and a very welcome encouragement was a sum of money from Hislop College in support of student and other youth work. George undertook the planning and the supervision and management of the building programme. The houses were of Sevagram design — two biggish ones for conferences, a library, etc., and three small ones, one for each family, all of similar build and size but adjustable to each family's wishes inside. We went off on furlough before our own house was built (we lived at first in one of the conference houses) and David took on the building supervision and the building of the Chapel. It was quite an undertaking, but the finished group of buildings was a source of quiet satisfaction.

All along there had been the discussion and planning of the life and work of the community. First and foremost was the question of economic witness. George had been convinced for some time that if he could do nothing about economic inequality, the Gospel would stick in his throat and he might as well resign — so there was some urgency about this. In the end, it was decided to have a common fund consisting of one third of each of our three salaries. This was used for daily housekeeping and, in view of the comparatively large missionary children's allowance, the fund would also assist with the Londhe children's education.

Manohar was in charge of the common fund, with Ruby in control of the catering and Alison and me as "assistants"! A village woman came to help – and David and George to

Oranges for a treat! Manohar serving rice and RubyBai the dhal (lentils)

consume and applaud! We all thrived on the Indian meals, three times a day, cross-legged on the floor. **We** were out of the red, and humbled by the economics of it. We missionaries gained **some** peace of heart and conscience by this effort. Always, of course, before our eyes, was the grinding poverty of the Asian peoples, which was not a pain we could alleviate in any way. I think the Allipur village people were happy and entertained to have us there – and one or two individual farmers were grateful for a pump in their wells and the developing services of the workshop.

Recently I wrote to David and Alison asking them to list what was important to them about these special six years. I have found their thoughts most helpful in focussing on the time, and especially on George's share in the project. I will just share them with you as they sent them. I have separated them individually to make a conversation pattern.

David: Being **in** India with the poor. Economic sharing — closing the gap between word and deed.

Alison: The sense of purpose — shared purpose and family fellowship.

David: Conversations about mission.

Alison: George's open, positive, cheerful outlook — his tolerant outlook which also set boundaries; and 'no' meant 'no' when he felt he was right.

David: The discipline of prayers, intercession, intimate, local, world-wide.

Alison: George's way of teaching which was clear, simple and confidence-giving.

David: Education about development; healing, farming, wells, co-operatives, industrial training, house and chapel building, transporting materials.

Alison: Enjoyment and fun. Small childrens' enjoyment of the life, children riding in bullock carts — their laughter!

Alison: Worship in the chapel, and nonsense songs.

David: Youth conferences, pastors' conferences, lay training.

Alison: George's certainty and (apparent) freedom from anxiety, so that others could lean on him when they needed to.

David: The beauty and peace of the place, walks in the evening.

Alison: The opportunity to share in village life and with the landless, in ways we could not have done on our own.

David: Opportunity for reading and writing.

Alison: The hospitality the Community offered although money was short.

I am remembering and picturing, and there seems to be a jig-saw — but not really a puzzle. I think each of us had one role we played mostly, but there was a great inter-mingling of gifts and contributions. At meals we sat in a circle, able to see each other, while at prayers and worship we sat in rows in the chapel. I remember that evening prayers were more informal and held in the eating place mostly, but in the chapel of course we were directed towards God, under-riding the family.

Manohar was concerned with worship and the conferences. He also was concerned with finance and management, but he assisted George in the leprosy work and kept it going routinely when we were on furlough.

RubyBai was mother-like to us all, and was responsible for our feeding; so she was of prime importance — and, like Alison, she also had her own children to care for.

My job with Ruby was to make chappattis (unleavened soft wheat pan cakes unsweetened). My great triumph was the day when her children ceased to hunt down the pile of chappattis in a basket, looking for the ones Mum had made — and instead just accepted one of mine when it came up! I knew I had won through! David's basic role was in continuing his Nagpur work with young folks in organising their conferences and in the organisation and planning of all the other study.

Alison's job was the prime one of "presence" — of being quite obviously a mother, with her own and other children. She visited village homes and made easy, pleasant friendships. She was available to help Ruby with the meal preparation and be with her and make Marathi conversation. The value of all these things cannot be measured but they can be sensed; so many people "got the message" (which is a very telling modern expression). George and I continued with our programme of four days medical work and there my contribution stopped. I confess, in hindsight, the medical work was more intense than I remember it later. I remember long days and exhaustion, and some migraine, but tremendous satisfaction and feeling I was taking my place with all the others in the jigsaw. But there seemed to be no such exhaustion in George. His "ideas tank" was fueled by a different energy and continued to produce various ideas in tandem with the clinic and all its demands. I think the six years of the Community represented a very happy and fulfilling period for him, although he did have an amazing gift for being content in whatsoever state he found himself.

The chapel was set a little apart from the other buildings. It was built of brick and mud, and wooden pillars supported the roof. These stood on the low wall that surrounded the mud floor on which we sat, and we could look out over the wall at the fields and trees. There were two reading desks about ten inches high, from which the services were led, and the communion table was made like a manger.

Allipur Chapel

The font was a brick stand with a clay water container. There was free movement of air over the low walls and between the wooden pillars — but there were no walls on which to hang pictures.

Surprisingly, we had two precious pictures — painted specifically for the Community by the Christian artist Vinaik Masoji, uncle of our friend Anna Masoji, present principal of Hislop College, Nagpur. He had worked at Shantineketan earlier with Tagore. Our pictures were in indigenous Indian

At Worship

style and they were very moving. They were large pictures, perhaps 3 feet by 2 feet. One represented the feeding of the five thousand with Jesus and the little boy with his loaves and fishes surrounded by the people and, in the foreground, the healed throwing away their crutches. We had it in the dining room. The other was of Jesus washing the disciples' feet — completely Indian. They were both very much admired. The feet-washing picture was in the library.

When we retired one was hung in Nagpur Cathedral and the other went to Bangalore to the Christian Institute for the study of Religion and Society.

There is one further rather remarkable Community event to record. A meeting of the **Iona** Community Indian/Pakistan Family Group was held in the Allipur Community! This was the second meeting of this Family Group — the first one was held in Nagpur and had a brief visit to the Allipur Community, which was then in its very early stages, but this second one began and finished in Allipur.

They came from Pakistan, from North, Central and South India. We had some children and a fairly new baby. A couple of missionary wives who had to cope with huge mission bungalows envied us our easy-to-run mud houses — and they had reason to envy us our showers!

We were 14 in all, including children. It was a momentous occasion. We had a fun evening at the end and gave an exhibition eightsome reel for the benefit of much entertained villagers — not to mention our own enjoyment. I have a vivid mental picture of George waltzing with the wicker chairs that had to be moved from one place to another. All outside in the balmy evening coolness and bright moonlight.

The Allipur Community was never intended to be permanent. It was an experiment. It was intended to be a pilot scheme of "community" that could be developed by a group of Christian people in any situation — e.g. in a village project, in a college or hospital, in a street, in a tenement close — we were thinking in terms of Christian vocation.

The community life never really seemed to flag, but gradually we "got the message" that we had fulfilled the purpose we had envisaged as a pilot community in Allipur. It became clear that Manohar was greatly needed in the parish ministry (from which he had been loaned for six years), and David was pressed to join the staff of the Nagpur Christian Council and be concerned with theological training as well as youth work. George and I continued where we had been, deeply grateful for the companionship of these years. George characteristically looked to see how we could develop some area of community within the small group of Christians in Allipur.

George wrote of this six year experiment in community: "This local community does not solve other people's problems, but a community which is learning to reconcile British and Indian in common meals, service and worship with families so different in income, may open a way for others. We do it because it is our obedience, our salvation, our joy".

What emerged in the course of time, after the Community period, was a less organised but still interesting use of the conference accommodation — occasional "hospitalisation" of mental health patients, often with some family; staff accommodation for the big surgical camp; nurses from the city hospital getting statutory rural nursing experience, etc. Many V.S.O.s came to us for a break, and there were a variety of visitors including, notably, several groups from the Church of Scotland Overseas Council, which we appreciated very much.

The three little family houses were reorganised. We remained happily in our own one. The Lyon's one became the small guest house and one of Doma's sons, Robert with his wife, Suhas, and their four children made their home in the Londhes'. Robert had a bicycle shop, and later became care-taker for the whole property.

Gradually, as we hoped, this loosely-held-together group took on a semblance and then some substance of community. Robert did his work and we ours, and Suhas was the king-pin and centre, the home-maker, as was appropriate. We provided most of the finance, Suhas provided the life and, reassuringly, one got the impression that she was serenely aware that this was so and acknowledged with dignity that there was no question of her being a servant.

George's own account of the Allipur Community is revealing:

Allipur Community is not a project so much as the

odyssey (series of wanderings, long adventurish journey) of one Scots couple, George and Mary More, sent to the Nagpur area, Central India. It is a lonely and unfinished journey and it is only reported at the request of friends.

"Allipur Community" is also a kind of confidence trick — there is no "community" to be seen most of the time. The "Community" consists of the risen and triumphant Jesus, the apostles, martyrs, saints of all ages and places, with varying degrees of assistance from the Mores, other Christians visiting Allipur, three local Christian families and sundry non-Christian neighbours. It is true that you might see non-Christian neighbours sitting in a church service or joining in a community meal but it is equally (and more usually) true that you would find all or any of them at loggerheads with each other.

Allipur Community is not a 'religious' community — it seldom has any outward appearance of religious cult. It simply regards the people of Allipur (6,500) and area (another 1,500) as a family. As they are all (except four families) non-Christian, and full of religious practices, the addition of an exclusively Christian set seems unnecessary. Salvation in India requires the abandonment of exclusive religious cult practices. If this is true, Allipur Community is well in the van!

Now for the tale.

Once upon a time there were District Missionaries who were usually Europeans "in charge of" large areas like a county or more and of such were the Mores. What they were in charge of was not clearly defined. The prevailing belief appeared to be: God, the Father, God the Son and God the Missionary. This was a comfortable environment for the new arrival, who was met with adulation — except perhaps by his colleagues. It was comfortable to his European background that he should be running something for the local people. This turned out to be a century old project called "The Mission", powered and financed by the European Western churches. While the aim of 'mission' was the change of heart that would mean forsaking sin and accepting Christ as Saviour and Lord, the method was education (expensive), medicine (expensive) and paid evangelism (expensive). The framework of 'The Mission' was The Budget. Outside The Budget there is no salvation.

After certain vicissitudes the Mores found themselves

with no paid teachers, no paid medical staff and no paid evangelists but still with the county of Wardha (half million of them). The local church was non-missionary. When it spoke it said:

1). Don't go out there, stay here among us.

2). Our boys are good-for-nothing layabouts, make them 'good', i.e. employable and marriageable (the order varies).

3). Clean up our institutional managements.

4). In a still small voice (usually as an afterthought) — origin of voice dubious — stay here and teach us the Gospel (they used to say "Preach it" also).

Many faithful people in the (Indian) Church look for the coming of the Lord; but the surroundings are cluttered with obstacles, bigger even than 'stumbling blocks'.

The Mores asked, and were given permission to, 'give themselves' to the village (then 4,000 people) of Allipur and its surrounding area. It is a self contained region about 10 miles in radius, tucked in a bend in the Wardha river. Allipur is the principal market town of the area.

Mary is a doctor (M.B., Ch.B. Glasgow 1939) who had originally qualified as a nurse. George was a minister (M.A. Glasgow 1939, B.D. St. Andrews 1947) with previously half a training in accountancy and five wartime years in the army. We decided this was all we could offer (i.e. no other paid staff) and said so to the village people. Of our qualifications the one most immediately relevant was Mary's medicine (there are still no graduate doctors in the area twenty years later). This was hard on Mary who, in the necessary legal employer/employee relationship, does not exist as a missionary. In these days she appeared as an asterisk against the name of the Rev. George More, District Missionary.

* * * * * * *

Missionary Children

We had — still have — two of these, one of each kind. One was born in St. Andrews and the other in Poona, bonding our two countries together.

One basic statement to be made, from our experience, about missionary children is that they formed by far the better half of our missionary team, in the early days, because they became so quickly utterly at home in India, especially so quickly at home in the village. Our foreignness was a great barrier in the village; the people were completely preoccupied with this, and with our possible salary and the cost of our car — a rather broken down wooden station wagon, in parts tied up with string! All of this tended to block the attention of the village folk to anything we were trying to tell them — of Jesus and His love, of causes of infant mortality, of treatment of leprosy, of cholera germs on the apparently harmless feet of flies, and in clear water. Janet and Alex went happily bare-footed round the village with their friends, in and out of the mud homes, joining their friends in collecting cow-dung to make cow pats for cooking fuel or to be mixed with earth and water to "do" our mud floors! Gradually there was a change in the village attitude to us. It seemed as if the village parents began to realise that, strange as we seemed, George and I were parents like themselves — that it was possible for ordinary human beings to look and act as we did, and the barriers did come down.

We attempted some "home teaching" for the children, but eventually the question of orthodox education had to be faced. Thankfully the days of sending missionary children for schooling to Britain at the age of six or seven years had gone. The accepted method in the 1950s and 60s, when we were agonising over the decision, was British-type education at the "hill schools" — many of them, but not all, American schools. Since American missionaries were almost double the distance from home than British ones, it was more urgent for them to organise the full educational course up to University level.

However, it was given to us to consider the possibility of sending Jan and Alex to an English-medium, but wholly Indian, school in Nagpur city some seventy miles from Allipur, instead of the thousand miles to either a school in the Northern or Southern Hills. In many cities in India there are "Bishop Cotton" English-medium schools, which the Bishop set up originally for the education of Anglo-Indian children. By our time they were simply English-medium schools run by the Episcopal Church for any child whose parents wanted English-medium education, usually because the family came from another part of India and the mother tongue was not Marathi.

We decided on Bishop Cotton school and the school hostel attached to All Saints Cathedral in Nagpur, but also that we would wait until Alex was seven — the magic Jesuit age — and so have them leave home together, as they had done so much together in their life till then.

The journey, to take them to Nagpur to introduce them to such a new life, I seem to remember being made in agonising silence. The greatest pain now is a realisation, watching them both in recent years with their own children, that we did not discuss and explain and ask their opinion or their concurrence. How patient and forgiving they were, I see in retrospect, for now they speak happily of that time. I believe it was a good time for them, but I do wish we had discussed and consulted! Perhaps it was just the way of our time — and the spirits of loved children are very strong.

Because of the many committee meetings in Nagpur we saw them frequently, which was a great comfort and joy. They were allowed home for the last weekend of each month. We felt they had indeed settled in happily when they announced one month that they thought they wouldn't come home next month — they missed too many things when away!

The Indian parents who put their children in the hostel did so partly in the hope that they would become fluent in English. However, I doubt if they did, because Hindi was the lingua franca in the hostel — it was the "National" language and the second language in the school. Jan and Alex spoke it between themselves for quite a time after coming back to Scotland when they had a shared secret! Marathi, the local and village language, was the third language in the school, and village-reared Jan came first in Marathi in her class! We were amused at that. On the whole they seemed to manage quite satisfactorily in school and were able to take their place at Jordanhill School in Glasgow for secondary education. In addition Alex learned to play, and to enjoy, cricket! This was an advantage when he joined the cricket-playing 69th Glasgow B.B. Company in Ruchill Church.

Educationally they both made us very proud. Jan went on to gain B.Sc. with Second Class Honours in Zoology at Glasgow University and Alex became Master Mariner (like his grandfather) with additional technical qualification in precision positioning, and most recently has been sailing Master off the coast of India, making full circle!

I cannot but have joy and satisfaction that Jan has chosen to be a missionary wife and mum — for that unique contribution to the spread of the Gospel. It was also, personally for us, a vindication of the life of a missionary child, in that she was willing to expose her own family to the experiences of being a missionary child, which she knew herself.

Equal was our joy and satisfaction that Alex followed my father into the company of those who "go down to the sea in ships and do business in great waters". Alex is very much a 'chip off the old

Missionary children at 1979

block' in that his basic life position followed George's — that is an interest in, and concern about, people. Further, surprisingly, he has followed George into 'community' for he is in the business of aiming at changing the conglomerate of a ship's company into a community — very much a Christian vocation.

Furloughs

Furloughs were an integral part of life of a long-term missionary. In the earlier years the climatic conditions made this long leave in a temperate climate a necessity. From the sending body's point of view, the missionary's speaking about the work done, the conditions and, above all, the people one lives and works with and for, all help to keep up the informed interest of the home chuch folk, which is a necessary element in maintaining financial support.

Reaction to this furlough business varies — judging by my own experience and observations, I would say the men accept it as a necessary evil and the women enjoy the social

66

and domestic aspects of it! George found the longer furloughs of a whole year in length a bit of a trial. It's an unnatural way of life to spend your time going around speaking about your work when you would much rather be getting on with it. In addition, George had a special horror of being over-publicised. This was a constant danger for him. In the first place, what he was doing was somewhat unusual and interesting and, worst of all, his wife was very fond of publicising it!

There was one extraordinary leave — it took place two years before we retired and only one year after we had returned from a brief leave in 1973. It lasted only one month and, thanks to the kindness of friends, we were able to take an Indian colleague, Mr. E. Augustine, with us. Mr. Augustine was the Partnership Secretary for the Church in North India and the Church of Scotland. All this leave of absence from work and considerable help with the cost was in order that George might accept the invitation of the University of St. Andrews to receive the Honorary Degree of Doctor of Divinity. Friends were insistent that the journey should be done and they would see that it could be done — and it was done. Indeed it was wonderful; all the dignified pomp and ceremony, the gowns and the mace, the very pleasant V.I.P. treatment, the dinner and the dance after!

This was the Laureation Address, July 4th, 1974.

"My Lord Chancellor, I have the honour to promote for the Degree of Doctor of Divinity, honoris causa, The Reverend George More, M.A., B.D., Missionary in Allipur, India.

"George More had the good sense to study at Scotland's two most ancient Universities. Instructed by the motto of one he has sought after a most demanding kind of excellence and following the precept of the other, which enshrined its guidance in a dominical saying rather than an Homeric phrase, he has followed Jesus as the way, the truth and the life. He has combined a tough, this-worldly interpretation of Christianity with spiritual stamina and a steady sense of vocation, formed by the discipline of the Iona Community and, since 1947, has brought this rare combination of attitudes and convictions to bear on his work as a missionary in India. He has chosen a kind of isolation from the great world and yet he has kept in close touch with it and has endured faithfully the contradictions which beset those who proclaim the Kingdom of God and know also the obstacles

67

which stand in its path. He is an intelligent and discerning observer of the world scene; he understands the political and economic forces which shape and move it and he does not seek release from the necessity of contending with things as they are.

George More, MA, BD, DD

"For many years he had aimed his Christian mission at all the facets of life of an Indian village and he and his wife have identified themselves with the concerns and needs of those who live there. He has sought to give substance to his vision of the wholeness of Indian life and she has helped him as a physician with her healing skills. His aim has never been to create a Christian sub-culture which would locate Indians in a Westernized ghetto, but rather to send them into the world and encourage them to be an agency for the breaking down of the compartments of Indian life and the creation of a more open and free society. The practical character of his approach to the village context in which he has worked is striking; a workshop engaged in simple engineering and the making of hospital furniture; a farmers' credit society which lends money to peasants at lower rates of interest than they can secure elsewhere; a medical clinic and a mental health clinic which rely on his wife's professional skills.

"This man and his wife have given a large part of their lives to the village of Allipur, sixty miles from Nagpur in the state of Maharashtra. We must on this occasion associate the physician with the theologian. Of his wife, George More has said: 'Mary gets nothing − a peculiarity which we are always too busy to solve'. They have lavished their combined talents and the rich resources of their love on an Indian village and

they have done it in the name of Christ. They have let the
world and its prizes go by and they have not grudged the
great treasures of their own lives. We shall sing their praises
in the congregation and give them honour which is their due.
We shall enrol George More with the great and the
distinguished and in doing so we shall proclaim that our
University is mindful of those of her children who combine
intelligence with goodness and who have achieved in the
world a kind of distinction which is not of this world."

Church Union

We were privileged to be still working in India when
forty years of hard preparation culminated in the
inauguration of **The Church Of North India**, in Nagpur on
November 29th, 1970, and we were present for the event. The
Church of North India was made up of the Council of the
Baptist Churches, the Church of the Brethren, the Disciples
of Christ, the Church of India, the Methodist Church, and the
United Church of Northern India (a previous union of
Presbyterian and Congregational Churches).

It was indeed a moving occasion, in a huge marquee
holding many hundreds of people. I especially remember the
organisation of the communion service which followed with
many Bishops, each with an assistant, placed at intervals over
the whole multitude. Being the Scotswoman that I remained
during all my 33 years in India, I was moved to tears by
singing "Pray that Jerusalem may have peace and felicity". I
stood in a strange place made of the Nagpur marquee and the
Edinburgh General Assembly Hall, and for the moment **lived**
the unity of the Church.

Presence, Piety and Pictures

Before attempting to round off this "second stage" of
George's life's work, I am going to recap a little by quoting
from an Iona Community article he wrote in 1953 "The Work
of the Community Abroad" — five years on and twenty five
still to go.

He writes much about the dilemma of Mission policy.
"How does the missionary fit into Indian village life? The
missionary has knowledge and experience which village people
need. We from the Western Church have a considerable
confidence in Christ's victory and present power over disease,
superstition and fear, over sin, evil and death. Every 'secular'

skill and scrap of knowledge and resourcefulness is valuable. All this can be communicated if two human beings can come together as neighbours, but the Indian village is far from Western life.

"The village holds much that is true and lovely and of good report. Amongst the most appalling indifference, you will find family love and devotion, honest work and men ready to give their lives for their friends; but the environment is deadening . . . . . few families can afford to buy milk for a starving baby. There are three overlapping tasks for the missionary who would help lay witness here:-

1). To find a point of contact.

2). To communicate all the good news (for the whole of the village life as for every person) serving with all one's skill, encouraging local leadership and skill.

3). To move on, for Christ waits for us in every village.

"The only point of contact is the sympathetic sharing of another man's life. This means living in a village and becoming a member of the community. A mud house is mentioned (of a Gandhian 'Sevagram' type) because a bungalow would be a great barrier physically (in distance), socially and spiritually. The 'rich man-beggar man' relationship would be automatic and damning. A bungalow would also mean the end of mobility for it could never be repeated because of cost. Sharing village life is unexpectedly rich and rewarding; and one of the delightful blessings is the change to 'Indian Time' in which watches and clocks (and very nearly calendars) are irrelevant!

"It is astonishing how much we from Scotland have to give. Indian Church folk, as well as Hindu enquirers, need much instruction in the Bible and the Faith but there are no compartments in village life. Amid such disease, as Christ commends, one has to heal. Different missionaries have varying professional qualifications, but all help to heal − by intercession, curative medicine, prophylactic treatment, public health teaching, by example and manual work. I didn't know when I left Scotland that I could design and build a house, instal a septic tank, make several kinds of 'human compost' latrines, design a clean well, arrange a pump for a shallow well, drive patients across country in emergency to hospital at night, face superstition and fear with no European nearer than 75 miles, help to deliver a baby, be as happy in the village with my family as anywhere.

"How long you stay in one place as a full-time paid professional I don't know. St. Paul (who often earned his own living) moved often and soon. There is possibly less skill in Indian villages than in Roman-occupied cities but basically the human situation is the same. I know only that not to move on is to fall away from Our Lord.

"The need for sharing the riches of Christ by sending men from country to country (in both directions) will **always** remain, but there may only be a few years left in which missionaries can enter India freely. In a period of great uncertainty and change, of re-alignment of policy and still continuing weakness, the Indian Church asks clearly and urgently for help — for India as a whole. The voluntary offer of independance has won Britain enough respect to keep the doors open a little longer. A vital chance to help the Indian Church to point India to Christ in an indigenous way is still open to us."

I hope I have managed to picture for you how George developed this insight and vision. Point of Contact, Service and Witness seems fairly straightforward. Urgency, 25 years on, is I think as he predicted — it was indeed urgent then but there has been, as he thought, only a few years remaining for free access of Westerners into India as missionaries. It is very difficult now to get the necessary visas, except for short term appointments. However, although the Church in India would still welcome colleagues from the Western Church, it has undoubtedly become a strong, leading, Church in the East and in the world, and still leads the world in Church unity. Along with the development of the Church in India, the whole East Asian Christian Conference and its constituent churches have developed in maturity and power and influence and what remains of 'Urgency' is in our need, in the West, to learn from them and from their writers like M. M. Thomas and K. M. Panikar.

But what of 'Mobility'? I know that George gave much thought to this and we read and mulled over the book "St. Paul's Missionary Methods". It seemed impossible not to stay put. Although he was not geographically mobile, I think George was exceedingly mobile in his thinking and in the variety of his service. Especially was his mind and spirit active in the realm of mission and the relation with other religions.

We were very happily part of a tiny Christian Church and family. When we arrived there was only one Christian family indigenous to the village, the only one remaining of a number of converts. Mostly they reverted to Hinduism. Doma and Vita Bai remained staunchly Christian through a period of some persecutions, but seemed accepted by the time we came. There was the 'imported' Christian family of the compounder, Robert Chavan and his wife Sharda Bai. In the course of nearly 30 years there were marriages and grand-children, producing a natural growth in the Church. There were only three baptisms in addition − of Hiraman and later his wife, and Leela who was of a new Buddhist family and had married one of Robert's two sons.

George used to like to point out the Christian contribution of service to the village − two trained teachers, two doctors, one cycle-lending shop, one District Council driver − out of the basic Christian Family. Doma himself had been a farmer and dealer in selling oranges in bulk.

When we joined the little Christian group, Sunday worship had long been established and was held in the Christian dispensary. All the Church's village workers were trained in leading worship and, in addition, Robert was a very accomplished linguist − in Hindi, Marathi and excellent English. This was unusual except in the more highly educated Christians. His fluency in English was especially remarkable, both in speaking and writing.

I seem to remember that discussion of the sermon material tended to be perhaps more in the letter than the spirit, but the singing was good and neighbours often came along and were made welcome. Our Christmas festival usually drew quite a number of our neighbours.

George would say to me "What really matters is our being here". I did not easily understand it then, but I was attracted to the idea, for I was beginning to question in my heart what was the legitimate aim of us as 'Foreign Missionaries' in India. I had never doubted that Jesus was the message. His friends love to remind me of how George said "When I got to India I discovered that God had been at home there for a very long time". Surely this is true too of the risen Lord − we are there to point to Him in that He is there, like the Kingdom, within us, all God's creatures, among us − this is our message. Just recently I had a flash of insight given to me. For many years missionaries have spanned the world calling on people to **change** their religion, join the Christian religion and have Jesus for their Lord. That is all right if they want it that way as, understandably, many Outcaste people do. The Hindu religion has gone badly off the rails there, although the Government has done its best to alleviate the unjust social consequences. Instead, should we not say "God has given you your religion and now He has come in Jesus for the world, for you and for your religion, to **change** it, yes, but only according to His will for it and for you. He will reveal your God's will, for there is only one God, and He is yours and mine and He came in Jesus for us all. Jesus' Gospel of the Kingdom tells us all of God's forgiveness, His love, His peace, His strength, made perfect in our weakness, His wisdom available to us and the power of His Holy Spirit — all there for us all because Jesus died for us all."

But, of course, that is only if they want us to speak of these things. In the meantime all we have available to us is to be 'present in the world', perhaps to awaken in others the religious question and to do that by our way of life. When the time came for us to prepare to leave India — we had had our chance and now we had to go; inevitably I was wondering "What of it all?" when a letter came from the headmaster of the high school to George saying that at their expense, they would like to have an enlarged photograph of him put up in the school office — and one of Jesus, to put up in the Assembly Hall! George went to speak to the headmaster, to point out to him that it was a good part of India that it had a secular state in order that all religions be equally respected in the country and none be given special prominence, but the headmaster said they were quite sure about it. They had come to understand something of Jesus and they wanted to put a picture of him in the School Assembly hall — and this was done. The picture was a poster reproduction of 'Christ in Gethsemane' by Heinrich Hofmann.

There is one more story I would like to tell of these finishing off days. Arrangements had been made for the taking over of the various pieces of work, all except the Women's and Children's Clinic. No medical person had come forward to take on this work, which had been a basic part of our life and service in Allipur. We had to prepare to close it down. We gave the patients their personal file number in these closing days; but said to them to keep it and keep an eye on the little mud-house clinic — for if it opened again, the number would 'work' — for we were leaving the clinic complete, in faith. There was in the nearest town a missionary order of Nuns from South India with a Belgian Missionary sister-in-charge. They had come to this Roman Diocese wanting to work in the rural areas. We had become friends with them, and they and we began the tentative persuasion of our Churches to allow them to take over our clinic. In the end we prevailed and we are still in regular touch with them and have news of the clinic, and of joint Christian worship. Jesus prayed that we all might be One. O that we could know it in Glasgow!

Stage 3
The Stage Of Vanaprasthya — Retirement

*'You have taught me ever since I was young and
I still tell of your wonderful acts"*

Psalm 71: 17

When George completed his missionary service in India and returned to live in Scotland, he thought of himself as entering the Hindu stage of life called Vanaprasthya, although he was well aware that the concept did not quite apply to his own life as did the first two stages. George went in for considerably more activity than is envisaged in the gradual retreat and detachment from life that is envisaged in the Hindu philosophy.

However, I believe that George persisted in the idea because he felt very strongly that, especially in these days of longevity, everyone should look forward to this period of life with eagerness and planning. He used to say that we were likely to have some thirty years in the first stage of education and discipline and general preparation for the life of the second stage in which we would probably spend another similar period of thirty years. Thereafter, we had to realise that we would probably have another long period of years to live, and should prepare for this realistically; not necessarily in detail but with expectation at the prospect of the wide variety of unknown possibilities. The important thing was to be aware and alert and expectant.

For all of us there are our neighbours — people of all sorts and conditions with needs, but also with a contribution to make to our lives. For everyone, there is the possible involvement in politics in all aspects and as a Christian responsibility. There is, at last, time available for the growth and deepening of our faith and our knowledge of other faiths and customs. We are privileged in Britain to live in a multi-racial and multi-religious community which offers tremendous opportunity for adventure and surprise.

Edinburgh

Within a few months of our return to Scotland, George was invited to spend a year in Edinburgh in a loose attachment to the Overseas Council in the Church of Scotland offices at 121 George Street, Edinburgh. It was in fact our last furlough year, and the most exciting furlough of them all! George was invited to help with recruitment, and was especially associated with the short-term appointments of young people overseas. He was also to be a temporary tutor at St. Colm's College in the field studies aspect, filling a temporary gap in the staffing under the Principalship of Duncan Finlayson, a friend of long standing.

It was very interesting work and a special privilege, we both felt, to be allowed to enter into this aspect of the overseas work − a round off of our thirty years service with the Overseas Council.

Duncan Finlayson wrote of George's contribution at St. Colm's:-

"I had of course known and revered George since our Glasgow University S.C.M. days. Then, when I came to work with the old F.M.C., I renewed friendship with himself and Mary, and stood in awe of their work in Allipur and the whole witness of their lives and their type of vision and understanding of what mission truly was. And so I was thrilled both for friendship's sake but also for the work's sake when it became apparent that we could have George temporarily, at least, as a tutor dealing with the Field Studies aspect of things.

"Of course I wasn't in the classes so I can't tell exactly what George said − how I wish I could have been a fly on the wall! It was immediately apparent that his influence was powerful and unique. The students never complained that the sessions with him were dull!

"I'm sure that some of the more 'pious' − in the wrong sense of that word − would almost be shocked by his attitude to some cherished ideas of the nature of evangelism and Christian triumphalism but they recognised that this was a truly holy man − so truly holy that they could not but acknowledge the sheer authority of what he taught. With all reverence I could not but think of what they said of Our Lord that 'He taught as one having authority and not as the scribes . . . ' − so it was with George More.

"He broadened horizons, he brought new visions to people of the nature of the Kingdom; he gave students a truer sense of proportion in spiritual matters, and practical matters. All this he did with a sense of Christian gaiety — positive jollity at times. How broad his grin when he would say 'I told them that St. Andrews gave me a D.D. for refusing to convert people to Christianity . . . . !' The problem with many of our students, excellent people that they were, was that their 'God was too small' — George More precisely met this need.

"It was just wonderful to have him in College in all kinds of ways and through him to have renewed links with his equally distinguished wife Mary. All through his life George was opening people's minds. Those of us who knew him realised how he extended the range of **our** thought and brought new exciting and fresh truths into clear focus."

In his accompanying letter, Duncan said "It was just his presence and deep influence which marked his time with us".

While that year in Edinburgh was a very satisfactory way of rounding off the thirty India years, in the event it proved also to be a bridge to the next nine years. In fact, in all the variety George had been blessed with in his life, there always seems to have been a thread of continuity — nothing in the new thing contradicted or negated the last thing, no matter how apparently different they might seem.

So I follow the thread back to India to recount that, during our last few years there, we were introduced to Transactional Analysis in the form of Harris's book 'I'm O.K., You're O.K.' and became first intrigued and then very impressed with the whole concept. By this time George had embarked on mental health work in Allipur and I believe his Marathi language skill was such as he could try out some of the T.A. approaches. He was really sorry that there was not time for him to pursue it.

We were still in India when we read that Dr. Archie Mills, who headed the Social Responsibility's sub-department on counselling and related work, had introduced Transactional Analysis into the methods used. We noticed that with interest, but did not envisage our being within easy access, being rooted in Glasgow. But, as you see, we were brought to Edinburgh and were privileged to receive a great deal of teaching from Archie Mills in that year. This was resumed, especially for George, three years later. Because of experience in mental health care in our last years in India, George had thought of counselling as a possible retirement work.

During this happy, privileged and profitable year, George was asked by the Iona Community to join the Resident Group at Iona Abbey. He did not think this was a really serious proposal because of his age and lack of recent experience of the Iona Community in Scotland. However, it happened that Wilma and Bill Stewart (friends and colleagues in India) invited us to share Shuna Cottage with them for a fortnight that summer. It was while we were there that Graeme Brown, then Leader of the Community, and Brian Crosby, Warden of the Abbey, persuaded George that the invitation was serious; that all generations were represented in the Resident Group. Since there were staff with children, why not grandparents?

George was not immediately persuaded that this was what he was to do. He seemed anxious about whether I would like it! I was influenced only by the memory of the support we had received from the Community in some difficult years in India, and it seemed obvious that if George was seriously being asked to serve in the Abbey, then he should accept; it seemed to me an honour. In the event it would prove to be that and so much more.

Iona Abbey

We took up our work in Iona in late December at the beginning of the Christmas House Party.

This was to be 'in at the deep end' indeed. This now traditional event was both a marathon and a miniature. It was a marathon of planning, preparation and performance, and a miniature of the whole life and ethos of the Abbey, set in the Christmas story. According to the Abbey basic tradition of combining work and worship in the Abbey, the resident guests were involved in one or other bit of the performance.

Some guests took part in the domestic scene, setting tables (referring here especially to the Christmas dinner table for residents and island guests), writing place-cards and arranging them, folding coloured napkins, and decorating the table. Others undertook the general decoration, formed a choir, led the worship and gave performances; another group was set to make the Nativity scene in the South aisle. That year it had a fishing village background with nets and barrels

Iona in the snow!

and the manger was a creel. All the figures were cleverly
suggested by grey blankets in the shadows. People tended to
be transfixed for a minute on first seeing it. The singing was
glorious and there was something of triumph in the singing of
us all.

The history of the island and the Abbey from the days of
Columba to the present day Iona Community has been well
and variously told and I recommend the reading of some of
these accounts. Still more, I recommend a week's stay at the
Abbey — a week amongst all sorts and conditions of folk in
Resident Group, in summer staff and in fellow guests. For the
fellowship of working together; in kitchen, toilet cleaning or
hoovering; for the elbows-on-the-table engrossed discussion
after meals (when you should be washing up); for the set
studies and the worship. There is a programme for the week
— the same each week, but different every time and for each
person — the Saturday evening worship which will welcome
you — you — not just one of the new group of 40 guests who
have arrived with you — the Sunday morning Communion
service — requiring five or more people behind the Iona-
marble Communion Table to serve the congregation from
Abbey, Youth Camp (from now on the MacLeod Youth

George leading the Pilgrimage in Columba's Bay

Centre) and Island cottages and camps. Each morning there is the Abbey morning service using the Community office, led by staff members — each evening has its own service.

Brian Crosby, Warden at the Abbey, had this to say about George's contribution:-

"What always impressed me about George was that, in spite of his universalistic open-ness to people and religions, he was utterly realistic and unromantic about people and their motives! He was never flustered, cowed or unduly impressed by anybody or anything and I could always rely on him for sound opinion and advice in the myriad situations that presented themselves daily at the Abbey. I think this was because George had truly allowed the truth to set him free; he had no axes to grind, no pretensions and no ambition, other than to be of service to others. What a marvellous colleague he was!

"In spite of what I might call George's toughness and realism, he loved people with a warmth that was immediate and obvious, and nothing is more important than that in ministry. It was, I think, as a counsellor and friend that he made his most significant contribution to the life of the Abbey (and to my life).

Liz and I both remember with joy his contribution to

George and Mary in the Refectory, 1980

worship in the Abbey; his fine prayers and his unequivocally radical sermons. It was always a treat to watch the faces of uninitiated people in the congregation as George pronounced sentence on organised religion!"

George was famous for the rather enigmatic, but attractive, 'fairy story' that he pressed upon us with smiling insistence. I have asked various friends to tell me what they made of it and I will try to form their hesistant descriptions into a 'statement'. George maintained that the physical tail remnant, which we all have, is evidence of the fact that we have personality tails through which we can express feelings without inhibitions. One is free to use physical movement to demonstrate the tail movement — with very satisfactory lack of inhibition, one can swing the 'tail' back and forth, or one can twirl it in complete circles, one can fling it over one's shoulder with aplomb, indicating that the personality tail is a serious part of our very selves. Understandably, associated with the foregoing, there was music which was unmistakably 'tail music'!

Perhaps the best way of giving a flavour of George's unequivocally radical teaching is to give the sermon notes for his first and last sermons on Iona, and to give an excerpt

Sermon preparation on Iona

from his sermon before the royal family at Crathie.

The first one he preached at Sunday morning Communion after his arrival on Iona, and the last one before he left, are on 'The Cosmic Christ' and 'The Victory of the Cross', and they were closely related. The first one very brief, urgent, almost like the announcement of what was laid on him to say — and the last one, restating it, filling it out so that no one could mistake the message.

The Letter to the Colossians was very basic to his thinking — Ch. 2: 15 — 'And on that cross Christ freed himself from the powers of the spiritual rulers and authorities; He made a public spectacle of them by leading them as captives in his victory procession'. Also Ephesians 3 — 'I pray that you may have your roots and foundations in love so that you, together with **all God's people**, may have the power to understand how broad and long, how high and deep is Christ's love'.

First Sermon : The Triumphal Procession.

Christ swept the board clean by his life and death and rising again.

1. Difference between Jew and Gentile gone.

2. Meticulous bondage to priestly law gone.

3. All our past sins and failure patterns gone.

We are free; new humanity in God's cosmic purpose in creation.

*Jesus is **now** leading a triumphal procession round the world; and in it, as vanquished enemies at his mercy, are all the principalities and powers that used to scare us into sin and death.*

This procession goes everywhere and is neither confined to Western countries nor to Christians.

Jews — Gentiles — Christians — others — the Christian Church, like the Jewish Church are usually on the wrong side. Rich/poor, white/coloured, imperialist/subject people, war makers/victims —

Narrow ecumenical movements irrelevant. Learning to join the triumphal procession of the Cosmic Christ who will call any people.

*Jesus' company is **not** religion — what's the point of another Gentile religion? Jews can join it, Gentiles can join — even Christians can join it.*

*Let's go and tell everyone the good news — Jesus has given us meaning: He has made it possible for us to live for others and enjoy it — He has ended the enmity between religions; **Anyone** is free to join Him.*

Last Sermon : The Victory of the Cross.

You will remember that Jesus taught us in what we call 'The Lord's Prayer' to say to God, Our Father: 'Your Kingdom Come' and 'The Kingdom, the Power and the Glory are yours now and forever'. When Jesus was with us He told us about the Kingdom and that the Kingdom had begun on earth. When He was crucified, a notice was nailed to the cross by His enemies saying (in three languages) 'This is Jesus, the King of the Jews'.

Kingdom, Power, Glory — we've all got ideas on that — we've seen majestic occasions on T.V.; we may have envied someone with power and glory! Here in the Bible we have two quite different pictures of the Kingdom.

Picture Jesus going to Jerusalem: Mark 10: 32-34 (RSV) 'and they were **on the road***, going up to Jerusalem, and Jesus was walking ahead of them; and they were amazed, and those who followed were afraid. And, taking the twelve again, He began to tell them what was to happen to him, saying "Look, we are going up to Jerusalem; and the Son of Man will be delivered to the chief priests and scribes and they will condemn him to death and deliver him to the Gentiles; and they will mock him and spit upon him and scourge him and kill him; and after three days he will rise".' .... and so it happened.*

Colossians 2: 15 (TEV) 'And on that cross Christ freed himself from the power of the spiritual rulers and authorities; and he made a public spectacle of them by leading them as captives in his victory procession.'

Since Easter, when Jesus rose from the dead, visiting his disciples to comfort them, putting strength into them with His Holy Spirit, Jesus has been what we call 'ascended' — out of human sight — until He returns to claim His Kingdom openly. In the meantime, to those who see, Jesus is walking everywhere in a triumphal procession of victory and inauguration of a new age which is both of power and peace.

This is the most important and joyful time there ever was. They've caught this on the West face of MacLean's Cross on Iona — and they've got it right that the cross with the risen Christ is **on the road!**

What is this procession and where is it going? Well it's going everywhere till everyone gets a chance to see it, and to join the celebration.

Who are the captives? Christ's enemies are the captives. I'll mention two sets only:

One. The bogies that frighten you to death — 'The ruling Spirits of the Universe'. Who are your bogies? Astrology (an interesting enough science) raised wrongly into a 'ruling spirit'?

Para psychology? Demon possession? Spirits who come and tell you what to do — psychic influences — 'I feel this and that' — with the feelings raised to the status of 'ruling spirit' — going mad? — the demon drink dressed up as alcoholism? Depression? Injustice?

All the bogies are there, captives paraded as powerless in Christ's procession in the full light of day. Don't ever be conned, frightened into thinking they won the battle with Jesus!

There's another bunch of captives paraded to be seen for what they are. They are the priests and rulers of all the religions who fought Christ and try to make slaves of us with religious laws. Annas and Caiaphas, the Chief Priests are there, the Pharisees, the Scribes and Sadducees . . .

But it's not only the Jewish religious establishment — it's the Priest-dominated establishment of every religion — Brahmins' power is broken — not Buddha could do it, nor Guru Nanak of Sikhs. The intransigent Imams of Islam are there.

Perhaps most shocking for us are the intransigent Christian leaders in the same company of defected captives — all who put a 'book of words' before the living Christ are paraded as captives. Many of our Christian establishments are anti-Christ — this is often true of the Presbyterians I belong to, and I believe it is true of others.

Who are joining the procession? Who are celebrating the victory and inviting all to join in? Christians? Yes — less the captives. But also Jews, Buddhists, Hindus, Sikhs. Anyone who loves Christ and openly wants to follow Him. Jews can join the procession as Jews: Hindus as Hindus: Muslims as Muslims. Christ's victory procession is bigger than any form of the Church we have ever imagined.

Chalo (Marathi) Come on! The procession is coming by — listen to the shouts of joy and release! Christ the King is coming!

Are you joining this Jew — our Saviour — The King of Glory?

While he was at Iona Abbey, George was invited to preach at Crathie Church and stay at Balmoral Castle. He found this an amazing experience, altogether pleasant, apart from the anxiety natural to such an undertaking. He reported that the royal family were most gracious and expert at putting guests at ease. I will quote a part of George's sermon:

*God is calling into being, as He always does, a people for Himself in Christ. He has no use for religion — if forced to choose one He would probably choose the Jews again, though He never wanted **them** to be a **Religion** — He simply wanted them to be a prototype of a work force: a company to do His work into which anyone would be welcomed. It is into this company that we are all called and, in turn, call others. Our greatest danger is that the Christian religion, with a powerful established church, will demand our allegiance for itself today in defiance of Jesus just as Annas and Caiaphas, the Scribes and Pharisees and Sadducees, standing for the established Church in Jesus' day, demanded the allegiance of Jesus and His disciples for their religion and had to be resisted to the death.*

*The struggle between exclusive cult-centered religion and God's regular concern for putting things right between people, has been on since the beginning . . . and it was a fight to the death! By not giving in to false claims — that the way of salvation lies in following the rules of **any** religion, Jesus **had** to be put to death.*

I learned by many experiences in India how God was present with all religions. I was on a bus on a hot-weather journey from Ajmer to Jaipur — about 80 miles. Dozing in the heat I slowly realised the bus had stopped outside a wall in open desert country. It was a temple. The bus conductor alone alighted and I thought 'Maybe he is visiting a friend'. Sure enough, he was back in a few minutes and the bus driver drove on without a word. Suddenly I realised I was in a communion service. The people in front of me, Hindu, Sikh, Muslim, had their hands held out and the conductor was giving them a pinch of coconut and sugar — the Prasad. Fortunately, I had time to see what was happening and have my hands out also, when my turn came — the only foreigner, and perhaps the only Christian — no words were spoken, no religion mentioned. We all knew that this bus conductor had ushered us into God's presence, that God had accepted us — each one, and enabled us to accept each other — as we were. No orthodox religion can enter this realm — for instance the Christian religion has plenty to say about things offered to idols! Was he ordained? There we go again!

Maryhill Old Church

While in Glasgow, we worshipped at Maryhill Old Parish Church. In the Autumn of 1983 our Minister, Mr. Cadzow McCormick, retired and George was asked to act as locum minister, 'until the spring' it was thought. In that winter, George attended to the, as he thought, temporary locum responsibilities and decided to put his main effort into school chaplaincy. He put a lot of work into this, doing four sessions each week. He enjoyed this very much and I believe was much appreciated. He thought it was harder work than preaching!

However, it became clear that the arrangements for the future of Maryhill Old were not going to be quickly completed, and George decided he must take the job more seriously. He helped the congregation, during the long vacancy, to plan for the future.

Eventually, after the linkage was completed, change and shortage of personnel led to George being invited to take the Communion Service on 26th October 1986 for Maryhill Old Parish congregation and for this I feel very thankful. In the following week several members stopped me in the street to say the service had meant much to them − they felt too as if the minister was speaking straight to them.

A week later, having received the surgeon's encouragement to do so, he took the service on 2nd November 1986 −

We sang 'Mine eyes have seen the glory of the coming of the Lord' and 'This is the day of Light', 'The King of Love my Shepherd is' and 'Who would true valour see' − substituted, at the organist's request, for George's original choice of 'And did those feet in ancient times' (Scotland). That was the last time we all sang together with George.

George died ten days later after apparently successful surgery. Something of his life and friendship is portrayed in the two tributes at his funeral.

> '*he,*
> *To whom a thousand memories call,*
> *Not being less but more than all*
> *The gentleness he seemed to be,'*

Tennyson, In Memoriam.

87

Walter Fyfe's Tribute at the Church Funeral Service

Indians describe some people as 'mahatma' — great soul. A great soul is someone who rises above the petty and selfish concerns of everyday life and adopts a broad expanded way of looking at the world. He or she remains calm when others are excited, thinks of the needs of the world when others narrow issues down to the needs of their own country, their own clan or political party, or church or family. They sustain and nourish the self-respect and the self-worth of people who are beaten down by hardship or poverty or contempt.

George was a 'mahatma' and Mary is a 'mahatma' and together, as we can see, they touched and blessed the lives of hundreds who are here and thousands who are not. It is not for me to frame an epitaph for George; his epitaph was spoken in his lifetime from the lips of people of many nationalities and many backgrounds.

When Elizabeth and I spent a happy week in Allipur we felt that the whole village were our friends. One man stopped George and myself in the street, insisted we go to his house for a cup of tea and brought out a naked toddler, his pride and joy. "If it were not for your friends", he said, "my boy would not be alive today, it's a miracle."

The Buddhists in the village told me they had wished to build a temple and had asked George to show them how to wire up an electrical saw. This was done so effectively and with such good advice that, when the temple was built, they made a good living as the saw-millers for the whole area. "We bless your friend", they said.

Two outcaste boys excitedly but shyly brought the latest metal hand cart that they had constructed, as they did with all their work, for the approval of the man who had taught them to weld and to sell their machinery around the area.

And when we were in Allipur, a couple came from Kashmir for their first visit to Allipur since they were married thirty years before. The man had been a stranger there, George and Mary befriended him and when, in the Indian custom, he wished to take a Christian wife, George was the messenger, the marriage arranger, the officiating clergyman, the matrimonial adviser — and here they were, thirty years later, coming to say 'thank you' and 'look how blessed we have been with your help, your advice and the example shown to us by you and Mary'.

These were some of the epitaphs we heard in our week in Allipur, epitaphs that did not wait to be spoken after death, and George, modest and diffident as he was, knew in what high esteem and love he was held during his entire life.

Another 'mahatma' among my friends, Father Borelli of Naples, when he was talking to young people in Gorbals, in clubs, he was asked by a pious Catholic girl who wished to enlist his aid in an argument she was having with Protestants: "Father, isn't it true that monks and nuns are specially holy people?", "No", said Mario Borelli, "everyone who lives is holy; monks and nuns are people who dedicate themselves to showing ordinary people wherein their holiness lies."

This is exactly what George and Mary have been doing for a lifetime, revealing to people, who can hardly believe it, that holiness is not the result of study or piety or alms-giving or prayer or membership of a religious community, but is a gift of God given equally to all people.

Since India was a large part of the life of George and Mary, I would like again to borrow an idea from that marvellous country. When Guru Nanak was a young man, coming of age, his parents arranged a great feast and celebration and got a priest ready to invest him with a sacred thread which would confirm him as a high-caste Hindu. However, to the consternation of priest and family, he stubbornly refused to wear it. He said "Let mercy be the cotton, contentment the thread, continence the knot and truth the twist. Oh priest, if you have a like sacred thread, do give it to me. It'll not wear out, nor get soiled, nor get burnt, nor lost. Blessed are those who go about wearing such a thread."

George and Mary have shown throughout their lives that it is not the outward symbol or sacred ritual that is important, but the quality of life, the living faith.

When Gorbals youngsters organised themselves into clubs, they came to us before Christmas and said "You know how Church people give money to the poor at Christmas, could we do that?" We said we saw nothing against it. "Who would we send it to?" they said. We said that we had friends in a village in India who used bits and pieces of money to help unemployed and so on, so a whip-round took place and they asked us to send it on, which we did. Almost by return of post came a letter from Allipur villagers. They thanked the boys and girls for sending on the money, which was being used and they enclosed a cheque, for when they heard that young Gorbals people were forming themselves into a club, they had a whip-round and sent over a Christmas donation. Thus a small bridge was built over a yawning abyss of sterotyped valuation of one another's culture.

This George was good at; he astonished charitable organisations who wished to send him large sums of money for use in Allipur, by asking for small amounts of money for an immediate project. He astonished radio journalists on his return to this country by replying to their questions on poverty in India by saying that he had not seen any. He undermined the sterotypes and he challenged the negative images, but never was George solemn. We remember him cavorting to Indian music around our Gorbals house to the great enjoyment of our children but to the great embarrassment of Janet. "Oh Daddy", she said, for she was just at the age when she thought that parents shouldn't do things outrageous or unconventional.

We remember the fun George had with everybody, including the elderly Hindu he told me about who found George jacking his jeep up on a stone that he found at the roadside. "That's our God", said the Hindu, and George realised he had picked up a wayside holy stone. "I'll put it back right away" said George. "No, no, finish what you're doing" said the Hindu, "he's doing more good for you than ever he's done for us!"

George's stories were great fun. We learned of his life in the army, of his University days, of his courtship and his missionary training, of his life in Wardha and Allipur, of his furloughs, including the one in which he was awarded a D.D. from St. Andrews. Remember he canvassed everybody's opinions about whether he should take it or not. And his retirement, that was another life again; Assistant Warden in Iona, locum and de facto Minister in this Church, budding computer operator, T.A. therapist, Labour Party treasurer, and Mary, doing all of these things, except the computer, and also being President of the Women's Section and working on the Theology of Feminism.

We are privileged to know people who have packed so

much into their lives, all of it to do with advancing society and helping people to grow and, happily, Janet and Alex, whose lives and occupations took them far away from Maryhill, were able to share some time with Mum and Dad, and George held all his grandchildren in his arms. The telephone kept in touch with South East Asia, the Antipodes and the China Sea.

As weak human beings we hate the parting from one we have loved so much, but we also know that eternal life, abundant life, real life is not simply life that goes on and on. It is the quality of life that is eternal and abundant and we know that our friend enjoyed eternal and abundant life and he shared it with us.

Jesus said, "It is the spirit that gives life, the flesh is of no avail. The words that I have spoken to you are spirit and life."

David Lyon's Tribute at the Crematorium Service

We grieve that George has been taken from us. We have been shocked by the suddenness of his going. It has brought us deep sorrow. We grieve, and how could it be otherwise? We have lost his presence. We miss him. But we are blessed, for to think of him, to remember him, is to have our joy pour in and the darkness of pain pushed aside — not banished altogether, but pushed aside. George always had the knack of letting in the light, wherever there was gloom or despondency, he let in the light, bringing joy and hope. To remember him is to be strengthened. In knowing him we have been greatly blessed.

We all have our own memories of George. My own stretch back over forty years. We met 43 years ago to be precise, when we were both soldiers serving in the Orkneys. I had taken a football team of the Argylls to play a Gunner team on one of the islands. I met George in the Gunners mess after the game. That meeting has stuck in my mind. I don't know why. I think we talked about what we had been doing in civilian life and what we were planning to do. At that time George was an ordinand, while I had no interest at all in the Church, and no knowledge of it. It may be that we talked about the Church — I think we must have. At any rate I remember that meeting vividly — although it could have lasted for only a very short time. The next time we met was in the quite different setting of St. Mary's College, where as a very raw Christian I found myself turning again and again to him for guidance. It was he who pointed me to the S.C.M., to the Iona Community, to the Foreign Mission Committee as it then was, all things that had shaped him. He shared his enthusiasm, and from then on for many years, he was for me, I suppose what we in India call a guru. I owe more than I can say to him. And many, many people here in Scotland, as in India, would say the same about themselves. George was the kind of person to whom people turned.

George had a remarkable gift of getting alongside people of every conceivable kind. I suppose I knew him best when we worked together in the village of Allipur in India – a very poor and backward village. He had an extraordinary influence for good over the 5,000 people of the village and over countless others outside. Hindus, Muslims, Buddhists, the very poor and the better-off, the sick and the healthy, came to him – and to Mary – and they worked closely together, one couple. George was always available and ready to listen, and their house was open.

George gave himself to the people of the village. And there was an amazing transformation in its whole life as a result, which would need a book to describe and explain. Basically the secret was that he refused defeat. He had a vision of what was needed to be done, and he worked at it until it was done. And he worked always with people, helping them always to use the resources that were in themselves, and were available to their hand. Sometimes the necessary skills weren't there in his village, and he had to acquire them for its sake. And this he did in a quite astonishing way. He learnt from books and by doing. He learned electricity from books, in order to get wiring done for electric pumps for irrigation; he learned from books about the use of a lathe in order to set up a workshop to teach basic industrial skills; he learned from animal husbandry books to rear buffaloes to provide butter; from books the care of poultry to provide eggs for the better nourishment of people; and from books he learned about the treatment of leprosy sufferers. And he did all this so that others could learn, and in their turn work for the enrichment of their neighbours and the life of the village.

He had a vision of God's purpose, and he held fast to that vision. And he had a way with him of sharing the vision, and of giving hope. To use the words of Paul in his letter to the Romans — George rejoiced in the hope of the Glory of God, and many caught that hope from him. He was an outstanding missionary of the Good News of Christ. He lived the Good News in his own life.

We grieve that he has been taken from us. We shall miss his supportive companionship, his lovely sense of fun — the chortle that was so distinctively George, and the twinkle in the eye — and his warm kindliness. We shall miss him and those closest to him will miss him most. We give thanks to God for the life of George, and for the assurance that he has passed into the presence of the Glory of God, and is at home in Our Father's House.

The One-ness of God

This is my prayer to Thee, my Lord — strike, strike at the root of penury in my heart.

Give me the strength lightly to bear my joys and sorrows;

Give me strength to make my love fruitful in service;

Give me strength never to disown the poor or bend my knees before insolent might;

Give me strength to raise my mind high above daily trifles;

And give me strength to surrender my strength to Thy will with love.

— Rabindranath Tagore

Teach me, O Lord to serve you as you deserve,

To give, and not to count the cost,

To fight, and not to heed the wounds,

To toil and not to ask for any reward,

Save that of knowing that I do Your will.

— Ignatius of Loyola.

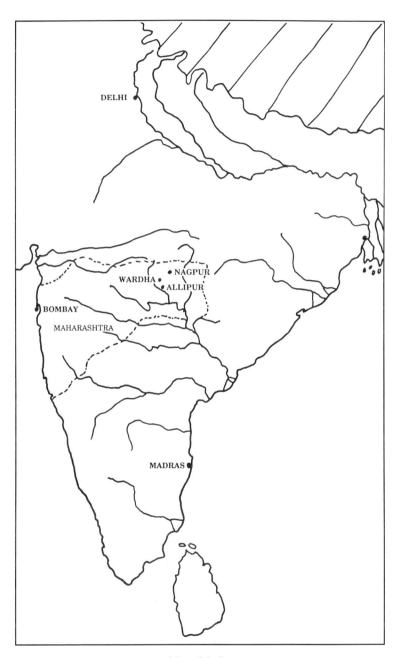

Map of India